Holiness:
The Beauty
of Perfection

Dale M. Coulter

Seymour Press

Holiness:
The Beauty of Perfection

© Dale M. Coulter 2021

Published by Seymour Press 2021
Lanham, Maryland
www.seymour.press

Originally published by Pathway Press

ISBN: 978-1-938373-56-5
LCCN: 2021939262

Photo by Dave Hoefler
Printed in the United Stated of America

To Esther, Bella, Sophia, and Christian

Table of Contents

Foreword

I have known Dale Coulter for many years. In fact, we entered a ministry partnership over ten years ago when he became part of the pastoral staff at the church where I served as Senior Pastor in Orlando, Florida. That ministry partnership has evolved into a close personal friendship.

Even from those early days of ministry, it became apparent that Dale had a passion for learning and communicating Biblical truth in a way that was culturally relevant and theologically sound. That passion has determined the priorities of his life. Over the years, I have often said to him, "When you write your first book... " I knew the day would come when what was in his head and his heart would find expression through his hands in the form of the written word.

In the present book, he deals with a subject that is often misunderstood and somewhat neglected even in Evangelical circles. With clarity, understanding and insight, he presents the subject of holiness from a perspective that motivates rather than intimidates the reader. An understanding of holiness is essential to our relationship with God and foundational to our call as Christians to make disciples. Throughout the book, Dale uses terms and illustrations that help the reader grasp the multiple aspects of the truth concerning holiness.

As I read chapter after chapter I found myself saying, "Yes," which in this context is the equivalent to "Amen." When I came to the final page of the last chapter, I found myself exclaiming aloud, "Praise the Lord" as I considered the blessings of a holy life. This book will transition you from thinking of holiness only in terms of a theological concept, and you will begin to view it as a transforming truth that influences every part of your life. Whether you are a pastor or a layperson, this book will encourage, enlighten, and enrich your life. I recommend it as an excellent resource for a balanced and Biblical view of holiness.

Shalom!
Bishop Mitchell E. Corder

Preface

During the summer of 2000 my aunt Lois came to visit my wife and me at our home in Cleveland. Little did I know at the time that it was to be her first and final visit. She made the long trip from Florida with my mother and father because she wanted to see our new house and also take a break from the daily demands she faced. One day we decided to take a trip to Fields in the Wood, a small park centered around the sites important to the early history of the Church of God and the Church of God of Prophecy. The Church of God of Prophecy operates the park and has constructed a variety of monuments dedicated to various Biblical or Pentecostal themes. Sometimes when you visit places that are part of the larger history to which you belong–as this place was–they conjure images of your own personal journey. At least, this was the case for us that day. As we surveyed the various sites, we found ourselves engaging in a conversation about the theology of holiness and the ways in which an emphasis on holiness had shaped us for good and ill.

When we started the car to head back to Cleveland, the conversation turned and my aunt began to share of her own experience. "I believe in holiness" she said, as we traversed the winding roads back down the mountain. She continued, "I remember going down to the front of the church and experiencing the power of sanctification in my life. I felt the presence of the Holy Spirit, beginning at the top of my head and running to the bottom of my feet. When I left the altar, I knew that I was clean before the Lord." Those words left a mark on me. What impressed me was the drive and hunger for holiness that hovered just below the surface of her words. As she spoke, I could sense a passionate commitment to pursue God at all costs. She truly exemplified the quest for the beauty of holiness present within earlier generations.

In this book, I have tried to recapture some of that initial passion for the holy life that my aunt had. It was and is this passion that caused men and women of our past to rush headlong toward the altar at the front of the church and hurl themselves before God praying and beseeching Him to fill them with His presence. They had caught a glimpse of something better than what they had. What was it that attracted them to holiness? I would like to suggest that they had caught a glimpse of the beauty of God's perfection and they yearned for their lives to reflect that beauty. Like a bride beholds her bridegroom with transfixed eyes, so they beheld the beauty of the Lord and passionately ran towards him.

Make no mistake, this is a theological book. To my mind, if we are going to rekindle a passion for holiness we need to engage in the sometimes strenuous task of doing good theology. Contrary to what some may think, good theology gives rise to healthy and whole lives. Like plowing a field, the work may be difficult but when the crops ripen, it's clearly worth the effort. Doing the hard work of developing a sound theology will produce a lifetime of good crops. Bad theology has the opposite effect. It can do serious damage to people. Consequently, I have tried to offer help in developing a sound theology about holiness.

There are several persons who read parts of the manuscript as it was in preparation. My thanks go to Drs. Jackie and Cheryl Bridges Johns who read several chapters. My former colleagues, Drs. Terry Cross and Todd Hibbard also read chapters and gave me feedback on them for which I am grateful. All of these readers helped to shape the material in the book through their encouragement and/or comments, which I trust has made it a better book. Finally, my thanks go to Bishop Mitchell Corder his constant friendship over the years. And last, this book is dedicated to my wife, Esther and our children, Bella, Sophia, and Christian for the beauty and joy that they have brought to my life. The song Esther wrote several years ago expresses well my own prayer: Show me your beauty in the rightness of your ways, show me your beauty in the sameness of my days, show me your beauty in the wonder of your face, then I will say that I am satisfied.

Chattanooga, TN
Pentecost 2021

Chapter 1
Why Forgiveness is Not Enough

May the God of peace himself sanctify you entirely;
and may your spirit and soul and body be kept sound and blameless
at the coming of our Lord Jesus Christ. The one who calls you is
faithful, and he will do this.

(1 Thess. 5:23-24; NRSV)

"I forgive you," she said.

"You do?" came the reply. Jim could feel his tense muscles slowly relax. All that mattered was hearing her say those words. This infidelity was the latest episode in a long battle to control his own urges and he needed to know everything was alright.

"I have forgiven you before and I'll do it again," Heather added. "The problem is not my forgiveness."

"I don't know what you mean?"

"Don't you? Jim, as long as you continue to behave this way things will not get better. Unless you change, all the forgiveness in the world will not be enough to save our marriage."

It may seem odd to begin with a chapter that runs counter to one of the basic aspects of the Christian message. After all, scripture clearly emphasizes forgiveness of sins as part of the Gospel (Acts 13:38; Eph. 1:7). In fact, it could be argued that the promise of forgiveness lies at the heart of the Gospel message. The truth of the Gospel is that God forgives sinners not because they have done anything to deserve it, but because of his gracious and merciful kindness extended in and through Jesus Christ. Without denying the importance of forgiveness, let me suggest that it only deals with a part of the problem humans face. God not only must forgive us of the wrongs we have done, he must also heal us of the damage those sinful actions inflict upon us so that we do not commit them again. When we begin to see how God heals us, we take our first step toward understanding why God calls us to holy living.

To explain why God's work extends beyond forgiveness, we should begin with an exploration of human sinfulness. In general, it may be helpful to think of sin as both a disease and as transgression. When we think of sin as transgression we are considering it in terms of a kind of criminal act in violation of God's laws. The New Testament writers describe this sinful act either by using the plural "sins" or with the language of trespass. James tells his readers to "confess your sins to one another" (Jas 5:15) while Paul reminds the house churches in Colossae that God has "forgiven you all trespasses" (Col. 2:13). This is how many people think of sin when they offer definitions such as missing the mark or disobeying God. Just as criminals incur guilt and therefore punishment as a result of their crimes, so sinners incur guilt and punishment as a result of their sins. Transgressions must be forgiven.

When we think of sin as a disease we are considering it in terms of an inherited and the internal damage our sinful actions and the sinful actions of others inflict upon us. Just as a disease weakens the body, strips it of life and ends in death, sin weakens us, strips us of life, and leads to our spiritual demise. Whereas a transgression must be forgiven, a disease must be cured. To understand why holiness is necessary, we need to think of sin as a disease in three ways: a self-inflicted disease; a social disease; and an inborn disease. Once we explore these three aspects of sin, the nature and purpose of forgiveness will become clearer.

Sin as Self-inflicted Disease

Paul's examination of sinfulness in Romans provides a good place from which to begin our investigation of sin as a self-inflicted disease. Following the prologue (Rom. 1:1-17), the opening chapters attempt to persuade the reader that both Jews and Gentiles stand in the same position before God. Romans 1:18 and Romans 3:23 stand like flag posts in Paul's argument in that the former opens with all are under wrath while the latter summarizes the larger point with "all have sinned and fallen short of God's glory." A central thread running throughout this section is the relationship between choices and consequences. Paul describes the descent into sin as a series of choices that lead individuals into ever increasing degrees of corruption. This is the self-inflicted disease of sin where each sinful choice warps patterns of thinking and behaving with the end result that the person actually brings about his own destruction.

The downward slide has its origins in what James Dunn describes as "misdirected religion."[1] That is, it begins with a failure to recognize God as God (Rom. 1:18). Paul also defines this failure as a suppression of the truth that God created humanity for relationship with himself. It would be overly simplistic to think that what Paul means here is that these persons did not practice the correct religious rituals. The fact that Paul applies the same critique to his fellow Jews in chapter two should be enough to counter such an interpretation. He is not thinking about individuals who failed to attend synagogue regularly or who did not say the correct prayers. Instead, failure to recognize God means failure to shape one's life in light of God's purposes. As one commentator suggests, "to acknowledge God as my creator means to recognize that God has a claim on me that no creature can make, indeed, the ultimate and immediate claim on my very existence."[2] This is the truth that is being suppressed by Jews and Gentiles. Jews who have the law and Gentiles who have a law written on their conscience both fail to shape their lives in light of the divine purpose communicated through these laws (Rom. 2:12-16).[3] The failure to recognize the Creator contains within it the failure

---

1. James D. G. Dunn, *The Theology of Paul the Apostle* (Grand Rapids, MI: Eerdmans, 1998), 114-19.

2. Luke Timothy Johnson, *Reading Romans: A Literary and Theological Commentary* (New York, NY: Crossroad Publishing Co., 1997), 33.

3. Ibid., 35ff where Johnson discusses Paul's argument about Jew and Gentile being in the same condition before God. See also G. Fee, *God's Empowering Presence: The Holy Spirit in the Letters of Paul* (Peabody, MA: Hendrickson Publishers, 1994), 489-93. Fee indicates that Paul's answer to both Jew and Gentile is to live by the Spirit.

to arrive at the truth as to the direction one's life should take. God alone knows the purpose for his creation.

For Paul, the problem of not living in light of God's purposes reveals itself in individuals choosing their own way. Paul's charge that they "claimed to be wise" (1:22) is an indictment of their choices about the direction for their lives. There is a false wisdom in preferring creation over its creator. This is the point behind Paul's conclusion that they "exchanged the glory of the incorruptible God for an image in the likeness of corruptible humanity" (Rom. 1:23). Intentionally referencing humanity being created in the image and likeness of God (Gen. 1:2) as though a temporal and impermanent reality can quench the thirst for eternity. When they finished making their choices they had inflicted so much damage upon themselves that they could no longer recognize the truth: "they exchanged the truth about God for a lie" (1:25). This inability to recognize the truth does not simply refer to the truth about God, but about themselves, their relationships to their fellow humans, and their relationship to the entire created order.

What kind of damage does Paul envision? It is futility in their thinking and having their senseless minds darkened. Paul seems suggest that a kind of self-inflicted blindness ensues from personal choices that both corrupt and produce further corruption, thus leading the individual to inflict damage upon himself, his fellow humans, and creation itself. As he declares in 1:28, "And since they did not see fit to acknowledge God, God gave them up to a debased mind and to things that should not be done." The self-inflicted damage

5

of sinful choices brings disorder to all the individual's relationships. The individual no longer lives in harmony with God, which impacts all of his other relationships. Paul creates a picture of a person no longer capable of relating to God, himself, others and even creation in the appropriate ways.

How do our choices to sin inflict damage upon us? Let's consider the example of adultery. When a spouse commits adultery, he or she incurs guilt for that sin, but he or she also inflicts damage upon their soul. They can ask forgiveness from God and the wife or husband and receive it, but that forgiveness does not completely repair the damage done by their action. Consider for a moment all of the thoughts and actions leading up to an act of adultery. A married person does not wake up one day and simply decide, "I'm going to commit adultery." The act of adultery comes at the end of a series of choices in which a person must entertain sexual thoughts repeatedly, must convince themselves that the wife or husband does not satisfy him or her, and must devalue their spouse to convince themselves that their action is justified.

All of those choices inflict damage by creating sinful patterns of thought and behavior. They damage his or her thinking, clouding it with lies about him or herself, his needs, and the spouse, and corrupting it such that they eventually give birth to the act of adultery. The deceptive nature of these patterns of thought and behavior is that they can begin with choices made while struggling through real issues that the husband and wife face in their marriage. However, in the case of adultery, the husband's or wife's response to those issues places him or her on a path that eventually damages him or herself, the spouse wife, the marriage and his children. This may be what James has in mind when he states, "But each one is tempted when he is drawn away by his own desires and enticed. Then, when desire has conceived, it gives birth to sin; and sin, when it is full-grown, brings forth death" (1:14-15). In this way, sinful choices can lead to sinful patterns of thought and behavior, and these patterns damage us because they produce self-destructive actions.

The damage our sinful choices inflict upon us cannot be repaired by simply asking for forgiveness, although repentance and forgiveness are necessary first steps. What we discover is a history of choices with adultery lying at the end of that history. It is the evil fruit born from a person's choices, and that fruit in turn serves to darken the mind so that the individual believes a lie. In this case, there are multiple lies including lies about himself, his own needs, his wife, his marriage, etc. Ultimately, the adulterer chooses to believe the lie that committing the act of adultery is really what is good for him. That is, only through an extramarital affair can he have his needs met, or fulfill himself as a human being. To repair the damage the person has to undo by choices all that he has done by choices. To put it in biblical terms, the adulterer is in bondage to sin because he has allowed himself to develop sinful patterns of thinking and behaving. The power that sin is given by virtue of a person's choices must be broken by that same person choosing through the Spirit's power. Repentance and forgiveness are the first steps down the long path of reversing the damage his choices created.

To illustrate the point further, let me tell you about a certain girl I know, let's call her Jane. This is the place where Jane finds herself. She is living with a drug dealer in an expensive apartment with expensive furniture. Does she mind living with a drug dealer? No, because he makes a large sum of money every weekend. Or, at least this is what Jane says. What about when the drug dealer hits her? This does not seem to matter as much as having nice furniture and a nice place to live. It seems that for Jane what is most important in life is having material possessions. As long as she can wear certain clothes, drive a certain kind of car, and live in a certain apartment, the occasional beatings, the drugs, etc., can be endured.

Now you might ask, doesn't Jane see how damaging that kind of lifestyle is? It seems so clear to us that her relationship with a drug dealer is not healthy, to say the least. But it's not clear to Jane. In fact, if Jane were here to today she might argue that she has the good life. It would be too simplistic to say that Jane sees the good life as having material possessions. For Jane, the good life has to do with the image created by all those possessions. It's the pleasure Jane derives from the overall image created by the designer clothes, the furniture, etc. That's the good life and maintaining the image requires a certain amount of money. Jane no longer seems capable of recognizing the truth about her situation. "And since they did not see fit to acknowledge God, God gave them up to a debased mind and to things that should not be done." There is a kind of self-inflicted blindness here, which in turn leads to self-destructive behavior.

Let me now clarify what I mean by the self-inflicted blindness that sin produces. Consider the difference between perception and reality. When we think about a person's perception of an event, we are referring to the way that person views what happened. The way a person sees an event--his perception--may be different from what actually happened. That is, it may be different from the reality of the event. If I were to look at a sunflower and say, "That flower has lovely red petals," my wife would wonder what was wrong with my sight. The reality or the truth of the matter is that sunflowers have yellow petals not red ones. Since my perception was so off, my wife would wonder whether I was going color blind. There is a difference between perception and reality.

Everyone has perceptions about life. Jane's perception was that the image created by material possessions led to the good life. The adulterer may perceive that adultery is what is good for him. But surely these perceptions do not reflect the truth of the matter. What we must recognize is that patterns of thinking and behaving create or shape the way we perceive the world including what we believe is good for us. The more we make sinful choices, the more we develop sinful patterns of behaving and thinking. Because our patterns of thinking cause us to interpret or understand events in a particular way, they keep us from recognizing the truth. To put it in another way, we become blind to the truth such that our perception no longer reflects reality. These patterns also cause us to misunderstand ourselves, our relationship to others and our relationship to our world. Sinful choices can lead to sinful patterns of behaving and thinking that bring a kind of self-inflicted blindness. This self-inflicted blindness in turn gives rise to self-destructive behavior. This helps us to see why Paul thinks that only by living in light of God's purpose or God's truth about ourselves can we really find the good life.

Sin as Social Disease

Self-inflicted blindness was just a part of the story for Paul. His analysis of sin in the first three chapters of Romans is not simply about isolated individuals but groups and group dynamics. Paul understood the history of Israel and the way in which surrounding cultures continued to influence the life of the nation. He employed the verb "to give up" or "hand over" three times in Romans 1 (1:24, 26, 28) to express divine judgment. The background for this verb is in the Septuagint translation of Judges, which employs it repeatedly to refer to God "delivering" the nation of Israel over to the surrounding peoples as an act of judgment (see Judges 2:14; 13:1). When Israel engages in idolatry by assimilating the practices of surrounding cultures, God "delivers them over" to those peoples. What is at stake is the influence of other cultures upon Israel over against the new practices God had given them at Sinai. Sin is not simply personal, it is a social disease embodied in the social practices and cultures around us.

To talk about God "giving up" or "turning over" people to their own passions and desires is not to invoke modern individualism. Paul recognizes the role of culture in the shaping of sinful habits and desires because of the role of nations in influencing Israel to turn away from God to idolatry. God's reaction is the same for society and the

10

individual within society. Judgment is simply turning people over to what they want. Underneath Paul's indictment of Gentiles is a subtle recognition that sin as a power uses the relational networks in societies to shape human behavior.

Every person enters life as a part of a family. The family to which that person belongs lives in a neighborhood that forms a part of a city. The city is a part of a region like Indianapolis is a part of the Midwest or Boston is a part of the Northeast. Finally, the region is a part of a country. We should think about each of these as forming a series of concentric circles with family at the center. As sociologists remind us, we learn who we are and how we should behave from the social networks to which we belong.

Choices to sin do not occur in a vacuum. We enter this world as a part of a social network, the most immediate example of which is a family. At the center of that family are a mother, father and older siblings whose choices remain intertwined with one another like strands of rope. The choices of the mother and father impact the children, and if their choices are sinful ones, these choices certainly damage their children as well as themselves.

The loss of a capacity to perceive the truth about ourselves is also a kind of socially-inflicted blindness, aggravated by wounds received from others. This kind of sin might be best understood as spiritual pollution because it has to do with the contaminating effects of the choices people make. Paul uses the language of "corruption" to get at this dimension of sin. He sees humans as "corruptible" (Rom. 1:23) and sowing in the flesh as reaping a "corruption" (Gal. 6:8).

Every choice we make affects those around us, and if they are sinful, we can be certain that those choices pollute and corrupt.

Let's return to the story of Jane for a moment. On the one hand, it seems that Jane's blindness to the truth about herself and what will really fulfill her seems self-inflicted. But if we look more closely at Jane's life we see that her perception of the world and what is good for her was shaped primarily by her parents. There was a decisive moment in Jane's life when she was with some friends in a fast-food restaurant enjoying a meal. As she was eating she looked up and there was her father on the other side of the restaurant. Jane went to say hello to her father only to discover that the man did not even recognize her, his own daughter. Her father had been on crack cocaine for a number of years, and the result of his choices was that, either out of his own refusal to do so or his inability to do so, he did not even see his own daughter. That moment burned something into the heart of Jane, it robbed her of ever being a daughter loved by a father, and taught her that she needed to steal up her own heart and become calloused if she were going to survive in life. Like dumping toxic waste into beautiful park, his sinful choices defiled Jane and perpetuated themselves in Jane's own life. "For all have sinned and fall short of the glory of God."

Although I have focused on more extreme patterns of thinking and behaving, there are subtle ones as well. How does racism perpetuate itself? Are children born racist or are they born to racist parents who communicate sinful patterns of thinking and behaving to them? In the recent past, there

12

were entire communities with ingrained patterns that taught their children to hate and mistreat others who were not like them. One need only watch a documentary about Rosa Parks or Martin Luther King Jr. to see how entire communities were given over to racism. And they were given over to racist impulses despite obvious scriptural passages like Paul's proclamation that in Christ there is no longer Jew nor Greek, slave nor free, male nor female (Gal. 3:28). Unfortunately, racism remains alive and well in our present culture. It is the result of the social disease of sin and the way in which cultural patterns pollute human behavior. Its continued presence reveals how the problem of misguided religion has more subtle versions that result in entire communities of people who perpetuate sinful patterns of thinking and behaving.

The fact that every person is born into a social context and taught what is important and how to behave in that context. Sinful patterns of thought or behavior can be passed along from parents to children. Sometimes children simply pick up on what their parents say or do; other times children are wounded by their parents' lack of love or attention and replicate the same behavior to their children. The same is true of entire communities that embody sinful practices like racism. All of this is not to excuse anyone from sinful behavior, but it is to paint a realistic picture of how certain kinds of sinful behavior emerge in people.

We must never fail to see how sinful choices pollute and pervert those around us. To pollute something is to defile it. When we wound others, when we pass along sinful patterns

13

of thinking and behaving, we are contaminating the spiritual environment in which we live. Make no mistake, this kind of spiritual pollution has toxic effects on those around us. It is one of the ways in which we perpetuate the disease of sin in the lives of others.

Sin as Inborn Disease

The social nature of sin and the self-inflicted blindness that it creates leads to an obvious question: how did humanity get into this state? What prompts people to make such self-destructive choices over the course of their lives? What causes parents to do damage to their children? What causes those children to inflict the same damage on their children? While I have offered partial answers to these questions, theologians have most often appealed to the idea that people enter the world at birth already infected with the disease of sin.

We can begin to get a sense of what it means to be infected with this disease by returning to Romans. In Romans 5:12-8:3, Paul depicts sin as an internal power that rules over people.[4] He describes people as "slaves of sin" where sin has dominion and reigns in their lives (cf. Rom. 6:6, 12, 14, 17). Sin also functions as an internal principle bringing a person into captivity (Rom. 7:23). These instances serve to reinforce the idea that sin operates as a disease warping the person's natural tendencies and moving her step by step toward destruction.

---

4. See Dunn, *Theology of Paul*, 111-14, for a larger discussion of this issue.

Paul gives us clues as to how he thinks sin exercises its control over persons. Sin attaches itself to human desires and leads them astray. It produces sinful desires or cravings that prompt persons to make self-destructive choices (Rom. 6:12). When Paul gives his example of how sin abuses the law of God, it is no mistake that he focuses on coveting (Rom. 7:7-12). The term used in Rom. 6:12 to refer to the "lusts" of sin and 7:7-12 to refer to coveting is the same: *epithymia*. While the term generally refers to human desires or passions, in this context Paul uses it to describe passions that have gone astray. Coveting at its core is misdirecting one's passions such that one craves something that belongs to someone else. As Luke Timothy Johnson notes, it is the "desiring disease" Paul has in mind and it applies to the craving after objects that are inappropriate.[5] If we recall that Paul describes God as giving persons who pursue their own cravings over to those desires (Rom. 1:24), we can see how the argument has come full circle. As an inborn disease, sin affects our desires turning them away from their natural courses to unnatural ones.

Theologians have understood Paul's idea of sinful desires to indicate that humans possess a fallen or sinful nature. Paul himself tends to use the term flesh as a shorthand for the compulsion we feel when our desires pull us in a sinful direction. In fact, the NIV translators decided that readers need to be told this is what Paul means by flesh, so the NIV translates the term flesh as sinful nature. The phrase sinful

---

5. Johnson, *Reading Romans*, 113-15. See also Dunn's discussion of sin as desire, which he calls self-indulgence. Dunn, *Theology of Paul*, 119-23.

nature communicates the idea that all humans are defective in some way. Their will and desires do not function as they should. Instead of desires pushing us toward God and causing us to make right choices, we experience just the opposite. Our desires work against us and cause us to make wrong choices. Every human being comes into the world defective or in possession of a sinful nature.

A theologian from the thirteenth century, Thomas Aquinas helps us unpack what it means to possess a sinful nature a little more.[6] Aquinas suggests that a sinful nature is a condition we possess in the same way that sickness is a condition. When a person is sick, his body cannot function as it should. The sickness itself is a condition that prevents his body from operating at peak capacity. Think of the effect that any disease has on the body. Diseases usually cripple the body in some way and prevent people from doing everything they could do if they were in complete health. Some diseases are more crippling than others. For example, Alzheimer's is a disease that slowly cripples the brain so that a person slowly loses her ability to think. In its most severe form, Alzheimer's causes a person to lose the ability to speak and function in other basic ways. All of these symptoms result from Alzheimer's attack on cells in the brain. A sinful nature affects us in much the same way. It is a condition that cripples us so that we cannot function as we should. Like any other disease,

---

6. Thomas Aquinas, *Summa theologiae,* 1a2ae. question 82. article 1. (trans. Fathers of the Dominican Provence in *St. Thomas Aquinas: Summa Theologica*, vol. 2 [Allen, TX: Christian Classics, 1948], 956-7).

a sinful nature deprives us of health. In this case, it is spiritual health.

We can get a clearer sense of how this disease affects our desires if we separate desires into two types. All humans have what I will call natural desires. These desires are fundamental drives that we have like the drive to eat, the drive to know things (curiosity), the drive for companionship (friendship) and the drive for sex. We call these natural desires "needs" because they are actually good for us. Anyone who has lost his drive to eat will soon die. The drive to eat itself is a good desire. Likewise, the drive for sex is vital to the procreation of children and the intimacy of marriage. Humans also have another set of desires, which I will call acquired desires.[7] In addition to the drive to eat, some humans have a desire to eat chocolate while others have a desire to eat pizza. We can call the desire to eat chocolate an acquired desire because it is a "want" we acquire on top of our "need" to eat.

The same point could be made about the drive to have sex. The drive itself is not bad. However, there are acquired desires like the desire to have sex with a particular person. The acquired desire may be bad if it is misdirected toward the wrong person. While natural desires help to identify our needs, acquired desires point us toward our wants.

---

7. I am taking the distinction between natural desires and acquired desires or between wants and needs from Mortimer Adler who uses it to explain Aristotle's view of morality. This distinction helps illustrate what it means to have a sinful nature. See Mortimer J. Adler, *Aristotle for Everybody: Difficult Thought Made Easy* (New York, NY: Macmillan, 1978), 83-91.

The problem of sin is that much of the time our acquired desires work against our natural desires. My desire to consume chocolate may actually work against me because it could lead to putting on a lot of additional weight, which in turn creates all kinds of health complications. This is especially true if I allow my desire to eat chocolate go unchecked. The same can be said for my desire to have sex with a particular person. Unless that person is my wife, the acquired desire can actually work against me such that I cannot have a healthy sexual relationship. The disease of sin manifests itself precisely in the way that our acquired desires work against our natural desires. To put it in another way, sin manifests itself in the way our "wants" work against our "needs."

I hope it is becoming clear how our desires work against us and lead us down paths that can bring about our destruction. We are moved by misdirected passions or desires to do things or to acquire things that actually do not promote our own well-being. Acquired desires create perceptions about what is good for us. The man about to commit adultery has an acquired desire to have a relationship with another women. His acquired desire leads him to convince himself that this is what is really good for him. As he gives into the acquired desire, it reinforces a certain kind of behavior. Enough reinforcement and the desire becomes more than a desire. It becomes a habit, a way of life from which the man cannot escape. In this way, sin becomes an internal power compelling us to do things. Sinful desires are nothing more than misdirected desires that we have.

In light of the distinction between natural desires and acquired desires, we can say that our sinful nature manifests itself when our acquired desires drive us in spiritually unhealthy directions. Moreover, we come into the world this way. We are diseased. Our natural and acquired desires do not work in harmony to promote our own well-being. We need to eat, but we want to eat chocolate (and some of us want to eat it all the time). We need to have shelter and clothing but we want to own a five-bedroom house and to wear designer cloths. We need sex for the procreation of children and the creation of intimacy between husband and wife, but we want sex for recreational purposes. As Paul would say, we covet and lust and strive after things. All of these uncontrolled passions or desires lead to murders, strife, adulteries, violence, etc. If we could get all of our desires to work together and to move in the right direction, then every choice we made would be for God's glory and our good.

Paul does not leave his readers to guess at the kind of destruction produced by the reign of sinful desires or passions. "For the wages of sin is death... " (Rom. 6:23), he claims. In fact, a simple glance at Romans 5 and 6 shows how often Paul links sin and death. Death enters the world through sin and reigns from Adam to Moses (Rom. 6:12, 14, 17). Paul describes sin's own reign as one occurring "in death" (Rom. 5:21), which suggests that the disease of sin both produces and thrives in an environment of decay leading to

19

the spiritual demise of the person. If the disease of sin is not cured, sinful desires ultimately give birth to death.

While much more could be written about the nature of sin, I hope that you can begin to see the complicate predicament humanity is in. As a disease, sin infects humanity in multiple ways. It is a self-inflicted disease because through choices we warp our patterns of behaving and thinking so that they become self-destructive. However, this is not the whole story. Sin is a highly infectious disease that pollutes our environment. The sinful actions of others contaminate us and can reproduce themselves in our lives. In the end, it is best to see this disease as in us from the beginning. It is the desiring disease where our desires work against one another and lead us down the wrong paths. Unless God cures us, we cannot escape the inevitable culmination of this disease in our own spiritual death.

Forgiveness and Salvation

Throughout this opening chapter, I have intentionally avoided any talk about forgiveness. I have done so because we need to see that forgiveness is not enough to cure the disease of sin. Many Christians just want to know they are forgiven without any sense of the need to be transformed and healed. They are content with a minimalist approach to Christianity. What is the minimum I have to do? For them, forgiveness becomes the sum total of salvation. This is not to say that forgiveness has no role to play. It is crucial as *one* aspect of our salvation. In a certain sense, we could call forgiveness the gate of salvation because it is God's invitation to enter his restoration program. As I said at the outset of this chapter, forgiveness deals with the guilt we have for sinful deeds and thoughts, but it does not cure the disease. When cut off from the larger purpose salvation, forgiveness becomes a form of cheap grace.

We can see how forgiveness opens the path to complete fellowship with God by briefly taking note of what people are guilty of when they sin. The guilt for sinful actions or thoughts does not reside in missing just any mark. Nor should it be thought of simply as disobeying God's law in the same way that a person disobeys the laws of a country. Ultimately, the mark sin misses is fellowship with God. The idea that God created humans in his image suggests that we were designed for fellowship with God. It was Adam and Eve's failure to see that the purpose for their lives could only unfold as they maintained their relationship with God. This was how they missed the mark, and, as Paul suggests in Romans 1-3, it is how all humans miss the mark. All sinful actions are reducible to the desire to go it alone and forge our own destiny without regard for our being created in God's image. Our guilt for breaking fellowship with God must be forgiven because this is the only way that we can begin to restore that fellowship. Forgiveness makes it possible for us to move down the path to complete restoration.

When ordinary human relationships break down, one or both persons must extend forgiveness. The break in the relationship created by some wrongful action committed by either party begins to be repaired when forgiveness occurs. To accept forgiveness means to admit that there is something wrong. Forgiveness opens up the possibility for a new relationship to be formed and for growth in that new relationship. The same is the case in our relationship with God. When we embrace God's forgiveness, we are admitting we have a problem that only God can fix. This is why forgiveness is the gate of salvation, but it is *the gate* and not the sum total of salvation.

Once we see how we are diseased by sin, we can begin our journey to understand why holiness and sanctification become crucial to salvation. Both deal with the healing of the person. As important as forgiveness of sins is to our Christian walk, it is only the beginning or the entrance to the larger task of completely healing us. Our restoration to God will only be finished when God fully cures us from the sinful desires that so easily entangle us. God's healing is nothing less than shalom, the restoration of harmony to the person with the effect of a quieting of the warfare between flesh and the spirit. We anticipate this shalom every Sunday when we see Sunday as the Sabbath, a day of rest designed to help us quiet ourselves before the Lord and rest from our daily struggles. Moreover, shalom does not end with the warfare occurring in the human soul, it extends to every area of life. The disease of sin permeates every aspect of creation. As Paul indicates, all creation groans in anticipation of its being set free alongside of the children of God (Rom. 8:21-23). Our task is to allow God to purify us, to cleanse us, to set us free from sinful desires, to heal us. This is the call of the holy life. It is the life that unfolds before us the moment we turn away from self-destructive choices and turn toward God. In that moment of recognition, God forgives and begins to restore.

Chapter 2

Fear Factor

That men may know wisdom and instruction,
understand words of insight,
receive instruction in wise dealing,
righteousness, justice, and equity;
that prudence may be given to the simple,
knowledge and discretion to the youth—
the wise man also may hear and increase in learning,
and the man of understanding acquire skill
to understand a proverb and a figure,
the words of the wise and their riddles.
The fear of the Lord is the beginning of knowledge;
fools despise wisdom and instruction.

(Proverbs 1:1-7; RSV)

I can still vividly recall the service in which I committed my life to Christ. It occurred during the middle of a series of revival meetings an evangelist was conducting at our church. On one particular night, the evangelist decided he needed to preach on hell and the wrath of God. He pounded the pulpit warning us repeatedly of the dangers of life without God. At the conclusion of the sermon, he decided to put all of the teenagers into a position where they had to make a choice. He asked all of us teens to stand up and then said, "if you want to go to heaven remain standing and come down to the front of the church." He warned us that if we sat down we were saying to God and the entire congregation that we wanted to go to hell. Well, you can imagine the kind of response he got.

No one wants to go to hell, and, more significantly, no one wants to proclaim to a group of people, "I want everyone here to know that I want to go to hell." The result was that every teenager headed to the front myself included.

When I got to the front of the church I prayed as hard as I could for God to save me. Although I had grown up in that same church, until that moment I had failed to make a firm commitment to God. I remember getting up from my prayer with the feeling that I was still in trouble with God. The next Sunday I returned to the front of the church again and pleaded with God to save me from hell and let me in his heaven. This happened about five or six times over the course of the next several weeks. I was terrified that God would send me to hell and I wanted some kind of assurance that I was really okay. It was only years later, when I was in seminary, that the assurance I needed came.

Fear is a powerful motivator and that evangelist used the fear of an eternal torment at the hands of a wrathful God to move me. The problem was that my fear did not go away because that night the evangelist had etched upon my heart a portrait of God painted as a divine judge who was wrathful and would not hesitate to send people to hell. Even after I became a Christian, I was always concerned about sinning before God. One wrong move could negatively impact my status. I did not want to lose God's blessing, or worse, my place in heaven, so I worked hard at living right before the Lord. My primary motive for living right was fear of divine punishment and my primary aim was entrance into heaven. I needed fire insurance. Just like any other phobia, I was intensely afraid of hell and, as a result, intensely afraid of God. It took me years to work through the "fear factor" in my life and the bad theology that accompanied it. Only after I changed my portrait of God did I begin to understand why he demands holiness from us.

Today, fear still functions as a motivator for me, but it's not the kind of terror associated with phobias that I felt as a teenager and young adult. Before we move any further in our discussion of holiness, we need to deal with the "fear factor" and the bad theologies that produce it. We also need to understand the right way to fear God and how fear functions as a positive force in our life leading us toward God and not away from him. Unless we remove certain ideas about fear, we will not rightly understand the purpose of holiness.

Fear and Bad Theologies

There are two types of bad theology that usually give rise to the wrong kind of fear. When these two theologies are in operation they can have a paralyzing effect on our Christian walk. The first I'll call worm theology and the second light-switch theology. Worm theology refers to any theology grounded upon the idea that believers should always see themselves as miserable creatures before God, no better than worms. This particular kind of theology was popularized in the 1700s and promoted through revivalist preaching. To move people to an altar, many evangelists, past and present, have relied upon a heavy emphasis on the idea that people are nothing but worms before God who stand in need of judgment. Not content to allow the Holy Spirit to bring a person to repentance, these evangelists feel the need to heap on guilt and condemnation. They combine the idea that God is a God of judgment who will not hesitate to send someone to everlasting punishment with the message that every person is so thoroughly sinful as to deserve divine wrath at every moment of his life. The suggestion that one is a worm before God has been used to compel even the strongest Christians to consider themselves as wretched sinners in the face of a holy God.

One can see something of this approach in the old hymn *Alas! And Did My Savior Bleed* written by Isaac Watts in 1707. The first verse says, "Alas! And did my savior bleed, and did my sovereign die? Would he devote that sacred head *for such a worm as I*?" Most hymnals today follow the version modified by Ralph Hudson in 1885, which is named *At the Cross* and changes the line "for such a worm as I" to "for sinners such as I." As implied in Isaac Watt's hymn, worm theology primarily emphasizes condemnation and judgment.

As a part of its over-emphasis on judgment and wrath, worm theology also specializes in the promotion of shame and guilt by constantly focusing on how wretched people are before a righteous and holy God. I am not talking about true godly sorrow for the sins one has committed. Sorrow and repentance have an important place in any Christian walk. Worm theology pushes the idea of godly sorrow to the extreme by requiring a person to focus upon how worthless he is. For the promoter of worm theology, God only receives the glory when Christians see themselves as vile sinners who stand condemned. The advice an English theologian, John

Owen (1616-1683) gives on how Christians should rid themselves of sin offers a good example of worm theology at work. He suggests that a person should constantly bring himself before God's holy law, reflecting on God's terror and how God will judge each and every sin. He states, "force your lust to face the gospel, not for relief but for further conviction of its guilt. Look to Him whom you have pierced and be in bitterness. Say to your soul, 'what have I done?... How shall I escape if I neglect such a great salvation?"[1] Owen initially does not want the believer to find relief in the gospel, but further confirmation of his guilt and condemnation. After these "general considerations" of the depths of his sinfulness, Owen directs the believer to focus on specific sins by noting how many times he has broken his promises to God and how close his heart is to being hardened. He states, "think of how your spiritual life has so often declined, so that your delight in spiritual disciplines, your obedience to His word, and your prayer and meditation have slackened."[2] These statements were written to Christians already attempting to live holy and righteous lives. They give a glimpse of the kind of focus on sinfulness Owen considers crucial if the Christian is to truly put to death the sin that lies so close at hand. For Owen, only when Christians load their own consciences with an intense guilt of sin can they begin to rid themselves of it.[3]

---

1. J. Owen, *Sin and Temptation: The Challenge to Personal Godliness*, abridged and introduced by J. M. Houston, introduction by J. I. Packer (Portland, OR: Multnomah Press, 1983), 175.

2. Ibid., 175-76.

3. For more on John Owen's views, see the discussion by Sinclair

There are several problems with this bad theology. First, *worm theology forces believers to view themselves always in a negative light as miserable creatures who should be condemned.* The focus remains upon detecting the hidden sin, the evil lurking at the door, the way one does not measure up to God's righteous standard. In addition, this intense focus on hatred of sin spills over into hating the sinner. In this case, I'm the sinner in question. According to worm theology, I should see myself as vile, worthless, no good and deserving of swift punishment. There is a kind of self-loathing here that results in a spiritually unhealthy lifestyle where the primary motive for doing the right thing is an overwhelming fear that God will send one to hell.

When this approach to theology becomes wedded to legalistic rules and regulations such as has been the case in the past one can see how easily it can damage our Christian walk. I remember one conversation I had with a part-time preacher about my walk with God. The conversation occurred not long after I came to the belief that God had called me into the ministry. As we discussed the challenges I might face, the preacher told me that what I really needed to do was remove the gold chain around my neck. The gold chain, he suggested, prevented God from anointing me and using me in the way God wanted. That preacher wanted to shame me into removing the gold chain by suggesting that I did not measure up to God's righteous standard (which, of course, included

---

Ferguson in his book *John Owen on the Christian Life* (Edinburgh: The Banner of Truth Trust, 1987), 125-53.

not wearing a gold chain). The result was that I wrestled with whether I was a vile sinner or not for wearing a gold chain because I was afraid of receiving God's judgment. The focus of my Christian walk became examining those areas of my life where I thought I did not measure up to God and, as a result, I found it extremely difficult to grow in grace. I came to view myself in a negative light not as someone created in the image of God, forgiven and being transformed, but as someone condemned and being judged. In short, someone who pursued holiness out of fear of punishment.

A second problem is that *worm theology produces a performance-based rather than a grace-based Christianity.* The only way many Christians can move beyond viewing themselves as worms before God is by engaging in a Santa-Klaus approach to their Christian walk. They keep their list of do's and don'ts and check it twice hoping to find out whether their naughty or nice. The list varies from person to person or church to church. For some, the list includes reading the Bible through every year; for others, it is having a daily quiet time. Still others think it means being at church every time the doors are open. This list could include not wearing certain kinds of clothes, not watching a certain television show or not listening to certain types of music. This Santa-Klaus approach specializes in compiling holiness lists and uses those lists to evaluate a Christian's performance.

Performance-based Christianity usually tends toward two extremes. There are those who think they faithfully keep their list of do's and don'ts. We'll call them the condemners because they tend to be the first to cast judgment. These Christians become the first to complain when someone else gets blessed instead of them. They wonder why God hasn't seen their supposedly good behavior and bestowed the blessing upon them. You can hear them say something like, "God, I've prayed regularly and I've been at church every time the doors are open so why have you blessed so and so and not me." The second-type of performance-based Christian tends toward the opposite extreme. We'll call them the condemned because they focus upon their shortcomings. These Christians think that they never keep their list and so tend to live under condemnation and in fear of God. Both types of performance-based Christians live with a constant nagging suspicion (fear) that they don't measure up. Condemners simply choose to focus on the shortcomings of others while the condemned focus upon themselves. While condemners and the condemned represent two extremes, the reality is that most performance-based Christians live somewhere between them, handing out judgment and yet living in fear of judgment.

Performance-Based Christianity

Condemners		Condemned
Quick to judge others		Quick to judge themselves
	(Most Christians)	
Wonder why God blesses others		Never expect God's blessing

There is a second kind of bad theology that I've called light-switch theology. Light-switch theology refers to the view that one can jump in and out of salvation as easily as switching on and off a light. The implication, of course, is that one can lose one's salvation quite easily. One slip, one wrong move and presto, salvation is gone. If someone makes a wrong move then he must begin the journey of salvation all over again. This type of theology can come in all shapes and sizes because most believers have different ideas about what counts as a wrong move. As I mentioned, some Christians think that even missing one church service without a good excuse can jeopardize an individual's status before God. The effect of this theology is that believers constantly think they must start over in their walk with God because they are always slipping up.

You can detect light-switch theology at work in a church where members constantly question the state of each other's salvation. Instead of the church being a hospital of grace where persons are healed and transformed, it becomes a cruel place where judgment and criticism destroy lives. In addition, light-switch theology also has a more subtle version, which usually goes hand in hand with the statement, "he's not in God's will." I remember one church member where I was on staff suggesting that the pastor was not in God's will simply because he was not going about things the way this member thought he should. The idea of not being in God's will is just a subtle way of suggesting that a person is not in right standing with God.

Consider how the atmosphere light-switch theology produces can work against our Christian walk. A focus on judgment and criticism leads Christians to question their standing before God constantly. They wonder if they are still in God's will and the object of God's love. They begin to say to themselves, "Maybe God's allowing this to happen to me because I'm not praying this week as I should." Their first thought is that God is handing out some kind of judgment upon them for their failure to maintain righteous behavior.

When these two theologies combine, it is easy to see the damage they create. Worm theology views God in terms of judgment and wrath and the person as a vile sinner. Light-switch theology suggests that a Christian is always one step away from judgment and losing his place in God's kingdom. While many preachers think these two theologies promote holiness of life, they actually have the opposite effect. Why? Because these bad theologies lead to the misguided idea that holiness is a set of rules and regulations one must maintain to escape hell and enter heaven. What lies at the center of both worm theology and light-switch theology is the same kind of fear I felt the night I ran toward the altar. This kind of fear is best described as being terrified of divine punishment. It does not create a strong relationship with God, but actually puts distance between God and the believer. Just like a person flees from a dictator because he does not want to be punished, so believers tend to flee from God.

The Beginning of Wisdom

Fear of God should not be equated with the kind of terror inspired by sermons devoted to guilt, divine wrath and judgment. Instead, fear of God evokes the healthy respect humans should have for God given the difference between God and creation. Yet, it is more than a healthy respect for God. As a parent I certainly want my daughter to respect me, but I do not want her to be in awe of me. After all, even though I am her father, I am a *mere* human just as she is a human. The difference between me and my daughter does not reside in our being human, but in our relationship to one another. How humans should respect one another helps us to begin to see the difference between respect for God as God and respect for another human. To say that we should possess a healthy respect for God has the added dimension of being in awe of God because God is a *perfect* being and not just another *human* being.

When we think of being in awe of God, we need to get certain common misconceptions about the terms awe and awesome out of our minds. You may have heard someone say, "that is awesome!" This use of the term registers some form of amazement at what has happened. Yet, awesome is so overused today as to have lost most of its original meaning. Awesome refers to someone who has been struck with awe over what he experiences. The term awe itself denotes a kind of reverential fear in the face of someone or something. I may say, "that is awesome" when I see my new bike for the first time, but what I really mean is something like, "I can't believe I got a new bike!" What I don't mean is I am struck with reverence and fear at the sight of this new bike. Since I teach college students, I can hear one of them protesting that he would be struck with reverence and fear if it were the right kind of bike. Some bikes require that kind of response. If that is the case, then I would suggest that the person really does not know what it means to be in awe of someone or something.

The experience of awe is more like standing before Mt. Everest and recognizing it's beauty, grandeur, and danger. When Isaiah sees God in the temple, he is struck with awe at the sight. Isaiah is not thinking, "I can't believe this is God," as though he could simply run up and touch and feel God to make sure that it was God in the same way one could touch and feel a bike. While a person might be surprised that he received such a wonderful bike, there is no apprehension in running up to it, jumping on it, and peddling away. Isaiah experienced God's majesty and power, which caused him initially to recoil. Even more than apprehension, Isaiah's feelings hovered between amazement and trepidation, wonder and reverence.

As C.S. Lewis says of Aslan the Lion, "he's good, but he's not safe." We certainly cannot tame or domesticate God, and a healthy respect for God keeps this constantly before the mind. So, by fear of the Lord I do not mean that God cannot be trusted, or that we must be terrified of God, i.e., I do not mean the kind of fright associated with phobias. Instead, I mean something like the reverence we experience in the face of something ancient, beautiful, and dangerous. Even the most experienced climber has a deep-seated respect for Mt.

Everest. Fear in this sense is closer to awe than it is to horror or terror.

We can unpack the meaning of fear a little more by briefly examining how Proverbs and Ecclesiastes both affirm fear of the Lord as the beginning of wisdom. In both works, the idea of fearing the Lord plays an important role in defining a person's relationship to God. Proverbs makes two overarching statements about fearing the Lord: "the fear of the Lord is the beginning of knowledge" (1:7) and "the fear of the Lord is the beginning of wisdom" (9:10). It also makes numerous references to the "fear of the Lord" (cf. Prov. 14:26-27; 15:16; 15:33; 16:6; 19:23; 22:4; 23:17; 28:14). While Ecclesiastes does not mention fear of the Lord as often (only five times), it uses the idea at key points even concluding with "fear God and keep his commandments" (cf. Eccl. 7:18; 12:13). In both works, fear of the Lord defines how a person should relate to God in order to achieve a successful life.

The question we must ask is what Proverbs and Ecclesiastes mean by fear of the Lord. First, many commentators suggest that fear of the Lord is a mind set or attitude that must be cultivated in the individual.[4] It is not primarily an emotional response that we normally associate with being frightened at a haunted house or something similar. Instead, fear of the Lord represents a constant way of

---

4. See William P. Brown, *Character in Crisis: A Fresh Approach to the Wisdom Literature of the Old Testament* (Grand Rapids, MI: Eerdmans, 1996), 28-29, 143-47; R. E. Clements, *Wisdom in Theology*, The Didsbury Lectures, 1989 (Grand Rapids, MI: Eerdmans, 1992), 60-64; and Claus Westermann, *Roots of Wisdom: The Oldest Proverbs of Israel and Other Peoples*, trans. J. Daryl Charles (Louisville, KY: Westminster John Knox Press, 1995), 128-30.

life before God. Second, if it is the beginning of wisdom, fear of the Lord must involve an outlook or perspective that produces wisdom. In other words, both Proverbs and Ecclesiastes promote the idea that "if you have this attitude, you will gain insight on how you really should live." Since this attitude must be developed over time, it cannot be an emotional response to God, a kind of fearful cowering as though God were about to unleash judgment. As one commentator puts it, "this is not the kind of fear that walks on eggshells."[5] Neither Proverbs nor Ecclesiastes teaches that the beginning of wisdom is to live one's life being terrified of God as though God were an evil dictator who hands out judgments based on his own whims. God is not Adolf Hitler, Saddam Hussein or Joseph Stalin.

With this general idea about fear of the Lord in mind, we can begin to probe more deeply into how Proverbs uses the phrase. The writer of Proverbs claims that to fear the Lord brings strong confidence and is a fountain of life that keeps one from death (14:26, 27). It also "leads to life" because it brings contentment and satisfaction (19:23). Just by looking at these few passages, we can begin to see that this is not the kind of fear associated with the terror of swift judgment, which prompts us to run from him. This is because fearing the Lord is closely associated with the idea of trust.[6] To fear the Lord is to trust that the Lord knows the best course for us to follow. Proverbs 29:25 illustrates this point well when it compares fearing humans with trusting in the Lord: "The fear

---

5. Brown, *Character in Crisis*, 29.
6. See Westermann, *Roots of Wisdom*, 129.

of man brings a snare, but whoever trusts in the Lord shall be safe." Proverbs 3:5-7 makes a similar point. "Trust in the Lord with all of your heart, and lean not on your own understanding; in all your ways acknowledge him, and he shall direct your paths. Do not be wise in your own eyes; fear the Lord and depart from evil." One can see the close connection between trusting in the Lord and fearing the Lord. Fearing the Lord brings a strong *confidence* that leads to life because it *confides* (literally, "to place faith or trust in") in the Lord to show the path to life. True wisdom comes when we trust the Lord rather than ourselves or others to reveal the path to life. This is what it means to fear the Lord and this is how fearing the Lord *is* instruction in wisdom (Proverbs 15:33). Consequently, Proverbs defines fear of the Lord like this: Revere and trust the Lord who knows all things and will lead you down the right paths.

If we examine Ecclesiastes, we can gain a slightly different sense of what it means to fear the Lord. One of the primary aims of the book is to investigate the seemingly utter futility or purposeless nature of life. Ecclesiastes is in search of a meaningful life, a life that is not in vain. As the writer puts it, "… all is vanity. What profit has a man from all his labor in which he toils under the sun?" (1:2b-3). The search for an answer causes the author to ask tough questions: Why is it that the wicked prosper as much if not more than the righteous? (8:14). Why does God allow someone to become wealthy and prosperous and then allow his wealth to be taken from him such that he has nothing? (6:1-2). Why are so many people oppressed? It would seem better if they had not been born (4:1-3). Ultimately, the writer of Ecclesiastes wants us to see that God's ways are mysterious. This is his conclusion. He states, "As you do not know what is the way of the wind... so you do not know the works of God who makes everything" (11:5). There are times when this truth hits home with us, and it usually occurs in the midst of tragedy or some intense struggle we must endure. During those times, we become acutely aware of the fact that God's purpose for our life remains hidden and difficult to discern. While we have an idea of God's purpose, we recognize that there is still much that we do not know.

How then do we find meaning amidst such apparent vanity and futility? One answer Ecclesiastes gives is to fear God. When one does not and cannot penetrate God's purposes for a tragedy one must endure or the particular season of life one is in, the appropriate response is a reverential respect for God. Another way to put the same point is that fear of God reminds the individual that he is simply a creature and not the Creator. As Ecclesiastes puts it, ... no one can find out the work that God does from beginning to end" (3:11). That is, even if you can discern the seasons of the year, that does not put you in the position of discerning all of God's purposes. As an attitude, fear of God helps humans remember that they are creatures who must stand in awe before the mystery of their Creator.

One can detect another hint at trust in Ecclesiastes' admonition to fear God. However, this is not a blind trust that confesses to know nothing about God. Ecclesiastes focuses upon rejoicing in the gifts God has given, which include wisdom, knowledge, food, drink and joy itself (cf. Eccl. 2:24-26; 3:12-13; 5:18-20; 8:15). Based on the New Testament, we could extend the list of gifts God gives to include all the blessings of life in Christ. However, Ecclesiastes suggests that even with all of God's gifts, the difference between the fool and the wise or the righteous and the sinner does not reside primarily in the events they must go through. Both experience tragedy, both can have wealth, both can be oppressed, both die (Eccl. 9:2). The difference lies in their approach to the events of life. The righteous live their lives in relation to God and this defines their character, which enables them to enjoy life's pleasures *and* endure life's disappointments. This is because, unlike the fool, they define their well being not in terms of how long they live or how much they accumulate, but in terms of the divine character they develop that brings them joy now and in eternity.[7] This understanding of what it means to flourish grows out of the more fundamental idea of reverence or fear for God as Creator. From reverence for the Creator is born a trust that the same God who gives good gifts has a final purpose that will be realized even if it cannot be immediately discerned.

Who is this Lord we are to Fear?

In light of the previous discussion, we are now in a position to consider the connection between what it means to fear the Lord and our conception of God. Those who stress the sense of terror normally associated with phobias tend to

---

7. Brown, *Character in Crisis*, 146-47.

view God as a kind of resident policeman or divine judge waiting to pronounce a sentence upon the sinner. As I mentioned before, this is where worm theology and light-switch theology bear their fruit, producing a theological poison that has disastrous consequences for the relationship between the believer and God. It implies that communion with God depends upon constantly viewing oneself as a guilty sinner for whom one wrong step calls down divine judgment. Herein lies the trap of legalism where acceptance by God remains dependent upon maintaining a certain standard of behavior. While the standard may differ from person to person, what links all varieties of legalism is an emphasis on God as divine judge and the resultant idea that the person must always appease God by acting in certain ways. A kind of servile fear, i.e., the fear a servant has of being whipped by his master, and guilt become the driving forces in this relationship robbing the believer of any joy because she cannot move beyond seeing herself as a sinner (worm) who stands in judgment.

John Bunyan, the famous author of *The Pilgrim's Progress*, tells a story the helps us to see how servile fear and a portrait of God as resident policeman tend to go together.[8] One particular Sunday he heard a sermon on the necessity of observing Sunday as a day of rest dedicated to the Lord. The preacher went on to suggest that playing sports, games, or working on Sunday was a great evil before the Lord. Bunyan notes how he left the church that day feeling quite guilty for

8. John Bunyan, *Grace Abounding to the Chief of Sinners* (???), ??.

42

his failure to observe the Sabbath as he should. The preacher's sermon led to a battle in Bunyan's mind that played itself out over the rest of the day.

After eating his afternoon meal, Bunyan indicates that he felt better and, ignoring the sermon, decided to play a game. While playing the game "a voice did suddenly dart from heaven into my soul, which said, 'Wilt thou leave thy sins and go to heaven, or have thy sins and go to hell?' At this... I looked up to heaven, and was as if I had... seen the Lord Jesus looking down upon me, as being very hotly displeased with me, and as if He did severely threaten me with some grievous punishment for these and other my ungodly practices." When this thought entered Bunyan's mind, it led him initially to draw two conclusions: 1) that he was the chief of sinners and that forgiveness was impossible; 2) if God would literally damn him should he continue to play the game and damn him should he not continue, since forgiveness was impossible, then why not simply continue to sin. At his own admission, his despair over being forgiven led him to desire to sin even more because he saw sinning as the only refuge from the guilt and condemnation he felt. Psychologists have described this behavior as a self-fulfilling prophecy. If a person becomes convinced that everyone thinks he is a horrible sinner, then his response may be to behave exactly that way. It is amazing to consider that in one afternoon Bunyan had lost the hope of being forgiven because he came to see himself in negative terms as a sinner about to be severely judged by a wrathful God.

It is important to remember that Bunyan felt guilty and a sinner before God for playing a game on Sunday not for murder, adultery or some clearly weighty sin. One can see in Bunyan's story the cycle of sin, guilt, and forgiveness the forms the legalistic universe. At the center of this universe around which all these things revolve is a misconception of God. As J. B. Philips suggests, we must see the idea of resident policeman as fostering an unreal picture of God.[9] God is not a cold and wrathful deity who is quick to make rash decisions or who is prone to outbursts of anger.

This false portrait of God creates other misguided ideas about salvation and the purpose of holy living. Before I was a Christian and even after I became one, I always thought that salvation was about escaping hell and getting into heaven–that was its primary purpose. Holiness was what God required of someone in order to get into heaven, and, in this way, it formed a part of salvation. I must confess that I did not always know why God required certain actions of me other than that is what God decided I must do to test my level of commitment, how sold out I was. Consequently, my initial motive for living a holy life was grounded upon a fear of hell and a desire for heaven that I equated with salvation. When one considers that the standard of holiness, that is, the test of commitment, keeps getting higher and higher, then it is easy to see how the universe of legalism comes into existence. Like John Bunyan before me, I was caught in a cycle where a piece of jewelry, not reading my allotted five chapters from

---

9. J. B. Philips, *Your God is Too Small* (New York: The Macmillan Company, 1965), 15ff.

scripture, or listening to a certain kind of music led to guilt, fear that hell was near, and removal of God's blessing (divine judgment).

This view of salvation and holiness leads some persons to think of living a holy life as being the opposite of happiness. They see themselves as having two choices: live a holy life now and delay happiness until you get to heaven or take your happiness now and forfeit it later. I believe this is a false dilemma. Holiness is more than fulfilling the necessary prerequisites for getting into heaven as though it's the equivalent of getting the required score on a college entrance exam in order to get into college. To see how this is case requires a rethinking of the false portrait of God created by the fear factor of bad theologies.

When Jesus states, in Matthew 5:48, "Be perfect, therefore, as your heavenly Father is perfect," he is not only telling us something we must become, but something that God already is: perfect. When we add James' statement that in God "there is no variation or shadow due to change" (Jas. 1:17), the conclusion seems clear: God is perfect and remains perfect. In fact, God is absolute perfection. The question then becomes, what does it mean for God to be absolute perfection? A theologian from the twelfth century, Anselm of Canterbury helps us answer this question by suggesting that if God is perfect, then God must be anything it is better to be than not to be.[10] If it is better for God to be all powerful than to lack

---

10. Anselm of Canterbury, *Proslogion 1*.

45

power, then God must be omnipotent. If it is better for God to be all knowing than to lack knowledge, then God must be omniscient. If it is better for God to be completely good than to be evil, then God must be perfectly holy. God must also be perfectly joyful and perfectly happy. When we put these attributes of God together what we see is that God is perfectly holy *and* perfectly happy. These two attributes must have something to do with one another, and, I would suggest, that to be perfectly holy is to be perfectly happy. God calls us to be like him, a being that is both perfectly holy and perfectly happy. Consequently, the path of holiness *is* the path to happiness. We cannot have one without the other.

To illustrate this point we need only recall the example of the man who commits adultery that I gave in chapter one. Once we see the damage that committing an act of adultery does to the man, his wife and children, we can begin to see why God says, "Don't commit adultery" (Ex. 20:14; Deut. 5:18; Matt. 5:27-30). God does not forbid people from committing adultery because God wants to deprive them of having fun. Nor is not committing adultery some arbitrary test God constructs to ensure the faithfulness of individuals to him. Instead, we must see the connection between not committing adultery and being happy in the same way that there is a connection between holiness and happiness in God. God wants people to have fun by keeping them from engaging in actions that actually destroy themselves and others.

The same point can be made about sexual practices in general. The moral principle of abstaining from sex outside of marriage is not about restricting the amount of pleasure or fun persons can have. It is about protecting persons from destructive practices that can produce unwanted pregnancies, lead to emotional scaring and prevent future healthy sexual relationships. I have a friend who during high school engaged in sex with multiple partners. Along with these sexual encounters, he repeatedly exposed himself to pornographic material with its two-dimensional portrait of women as objects to be used for personal pleasure and instant gratification. In his senior year, he became a Christian and felt God call him into the ministry. He thought that he should prepare to fulfill God's calling as best as he could, so he decided to attend a Christian college.

While in college he began to date his future wife. What he discovered during their courtship was that all of his sexual encounters in high school and his exposure to pornographic materials had shaped the way he perceived women and were now preventing him from having a healthy relationship with her. By his own admission, he could not see all of her wonderful qualities because his previous behavior had conditioned him (a pattern of thinking and behaving) to treat women as objects by valuing only the physical characteristics they did or did not possess. He once exclaimed, "God, she can't be the one: her breasts aren't big enough!" With God's help, he had to unlearn the mindset created by just a few short years of engaging in illicit sexual actions and relearn the appropriate way to treat women. Only after moving beyond the fantasized world created by pornographic images, was he prepared to handle the mountains and valleys that foster the joy of marriage. Abstaining from sex outside of marriage protects persons from actions that are not good for them or others to whom they will become married.

Holiness is not a set an arbitrary commands designed to test one's loyalty to God. God calls persons to holiness because God knows that if we are to be happy, then we must be holy. Holiness and happiness are a part of the perfect being of God. They are not separate from one another, but intimately bound together. As I said before, this implies that the path *of* holiness is the path *to* happiness: the good life. *True* fear of the Lord is the beginning of wisdom because it recognizes that God is our creator, and as our creator God knows best what makes us happy.

Up to this point, I have talked about holiness as being fun, but I think that we can now see that holiness is about so much more than having a fun life. It is about having the good life, the life that flourishes and prospers. In addition, while we stand in awe of God as a perfect being, we should not cower before Him in terror. God is not a resident policeman waiting for us to make a wrong move so that He can slap the cuffs on us and send us off to a place of torment. To pursue holiness with intense passion we must move beyond this false portrait of God and the kind of servile fear it produces. Our teaching and preaching should focus on a loving God who demands holiness because God knows that it is the only way to flourish and prosper as a human being. The implication of this idea, of course, is that sanctification lies at the heart of salvation and cannot be seen as an add on after conversion.

Chapter 3
Sanctification: The Heart of Salvation

One thing I asked of the LORD,
that will I seek after
to live in the house of the LORD
all the days of my life,
to behold the beauty of the LORD,
and to inquire in his temple.

(Psalm 27.4)

Many Christians equate salvation with forgiveness of sins because they are primarily concerned about getting into heaven. It is as though getting into heaven and occupying a mansion somewhere in glory were the sum total of salvation. This understanding of salvation shapes how Christians view holiness. When associated with "just making it in," the word holiness conjures up ideas about following a set of laws or regulations as the means of maintaining moral purity before God without which a person could not enter heaven. The ultimate point of following these regulations would be to remain in God's favor. Moreover, such a view of salvation usually gives rise to the worm and light-switch theologies I discussed in the previous chapter. This approach misses the larger purpose of salvation ,which is transformation of the person into a child of God so that she can reach her complete potential in union and fellowship with God. By reducing salvation to entering heaven and escaping hell, holiness

51

becomes more a test of one's loyalty to God than a real transformation. What we need to ask ourselves is whether holiness is about demonstrating loyalty to God, some series of tests we must pass, or whether it is something else. How should we think about holiness and sanctification? What is their ultimate purpose? These are the questions I would like to address in this chapter. By offering an answer to them, it is my hope that we will begin to see how sanctification is the heart of salvation.

Adoption: Making *Real* Sons and Daughters

Let's begin our discussion by looking at Paul's use of adoption to describe salvation. Paul writes to the Galatians, "But when the fullness of time had come, God sent forth His Son, born of a woman, born under the law, to redeem those who were under the law, that we might receive the adoption as sons. And because you are sons, God has sent forth the Spirit of His Son into your hears, crying out 'Abba, Father!'" (4:4-6). In this passage, Paul provides a nice summary of the work of Christ and the Spirit in making believers children of God. It is no mistake that he uses the same verb to describe what God is doing. God is *sending forth* his Son and the Spirit of his Son to bring about our adoption.[1] The parallelism between the Son and the Spirit comes out when one places the verses side by side:

---

1. See Fee's discussion of this passage from which I am partially drawing. Fee, *God's Empowering Presence*, 398-412.

(4-5) God *sent forth* his Son
    born of a woman
    born under the law
        to redeem those under the law
        that we might receive adoption as sons

(6) God *sent forth* the Spirit of his Son in our hearts
    because we are sons
    crying out "Abba Father!"

In this brief passage, Paul describes the work of Christ on the cross and the work of the Spirit in the heart as the two sides of human salvation. Both are necessary for adoption. The death of Christ "redeems" humanity from slavery to the disease of sin (the inward power at work in humans). It is a freedom from the enslavement to a way of living that is self-destructive and brings about one's own death. When we become a joint-heir with Christ, we leave behind the bonds of slavery and enter into a new life as God's child. One could say that the freedom of the children of God is their receiving the freedom of the one Son of God. As we participate in Christ's death, we enter into a new way of living whereby we experience the true liberty of children.

For Paul, our liberation is an *experience* because we cry out, "God you are my Father!" by the Spirit of God's Son who is sent into our hearts to confirm our adoption. Those who experience the Spirit of God, experience life in the Son. Imagine an orphan being adopted into a family where she experiences the warmth of love and acceptance for the first time. Her life is no longer determined by the rules of "the world" or some system of slavery. She ceases to be an outcast, an object of scorn to be mistreated and to mistreat others, but now forms a part of a new family structure. Through Christ and the Spirit each believer is adopted into the family of God and experiences the liberty of a new family life.

While, in an important way, the adoption of believers is complete, there is another sense in which it still must be completed. Adoption is complete in that through Christ and the Spirit each person is made fully a part of the family of God. However, there is another step. Paul does not conclude his discussion with this dimension of adoption. Instead, he asserts that what now matters for the adopted child is "faith working through love" (Gal. 5:6), which he will later identify as "walking by the Spirit" (5:16ff). Adoption into the family of God is the opening up of a new way of life that must now be fully actualized. The complete freedom of the sons and daughters of God is found only in the complete liberty from the desire of the flesh. As Fee suggests, when Paul mentions desire of the flesh he is referring to "the basic perspective of life in the flesh."[2] In light of chapter one, we could say that the Spirit is at work in believers liberating them from patterns of thinking and behaving that kill and destroy. The basic perspective of life in the flesh, or what the Gospel of John sometimes calls "the world," serves to enslave individuals. If the "adopted" sons and daughters of God are to realize their complete freedom from the world's slavery, they must walk in the Spirit. It is only through the Spirit that they will fully complete their adoption into the family of God because only

---

2. Ibid., 432.

54

the Spirit will form Christ in them and so make them like Christ.

These two aspects of adoption might be better understood if we consider how adoption works today. In modern society adoption usually encompasses two different dimensions that we could call phases. The first phase of adoption involves the parents making application to adopt a child and sorting through the legal matters pertaining to the adoption. This phase is a necessary step to guarantee that the adopted child legally belongs to the parents and hence has a rightful claim to be an heir. Even if the child is adopted into a family with natural children, he should have a legal claim to his parents' estate after they die. Upon completion of the legal phase, the child becomes a legal heir entitled to everything his parents possess. In one sense, Paul refers to believers being adopted children of God as those who belong to God and are now entitled to all that God has. For Paul, this adoption flows to us through the Sonship of Christ and is experienced by us through the Spirit being sent into our hearts. The Spirit is God's "down payment" upon our lives such that we have become joint-heirs with his own Son, Jesus Christ. Christ is the natural Son of God while believers are adopted sons and daughters of God. This is how Christians initially become adopted into the family of God. Because we are united to Christ, the eternal Son by the Holy Spirit, we share in Christ's Sonship and become joint-heirs with him.

While crucial to adoption, the legal phase must give way to the second phase, which concerns fully forming the new relationship that has been created. We could call this formation of a new relationship the relational phase, since it speaks to what the child and the parents must now do. A child's being adopted into a family requires that the child *adjust* to the new family life even as the family adjusts to the child. The child must learn to love his new parents even as they learn to love him. This is especially the case with orphans who are adopted at an older age. Once the legal phase is complete, an orphan is no longer parentless and he can truly say for the first time, "You're my mom and dad." When an orphan calls his parents mom and dad for the first time, it represents a new commitment on his part to be a member of this family. However, he still does not *fully* love his parents. He is their *legal* son, but he must become their *real* son, which requires that he work hard at forming this new relationship.

There is an important difference between being a legal son or daughter and being a real son or daughter. A legal son is entitled to all that a natural child has including the privilege to call his parents mom and dad. He has this new privilege because a husband and wife have chosen to make him a part of their family. What if the son did not seek to develop a relationship with his new parents? Would he really be their son? Certainly, in the eyes of the court he would still be their son, but without the relational bonds of love any legal bond would seem to be inconsequential. To become their son in the fullest sense he has to develop the new relationship. This requires that he change and grow and ultimately be transformed. He must adapt and adjust to life with this new family such that he truly learns to love his parents. While he might begin his adoption into this new family as their *legal* son, he must continue to develop the relationship such that he becomes their *real* son. It is only as the relationship grows and develops that he can say with all of the comfort and assurance of a child, "I love you mom and dad." It is only after the relationship grows and matures that he can say with the respect of a child, "I trust your decisions about my welfare."

At some point during their lives, most children have a sudden realization that they are more like their parents than they would ever dare admit. They realize how much of their lives have been transformed by their parents' influence. This was certainly the case with me. The characteristics of my father and mother have become, in part, my own characteristics. My father loves to have something sweet after a meal, even a simple taste will due. Like him, I find myself desiring to have that same experience of tasting some sugary substance as it moves past the lips onto the tongue and, swirling around in a liquefied mass of utter delight, finally makes a conclusive descent into the stomach. I have also discovered that I share the same sentimentality as my father. He cries very easily and finds items conjuring nostalgic feelings where others only see junk; traits at times too familiar for my own comfort. I fight his battles, wrestling in my soul with the doubt and despair I so often saw him contending against in our small home. Although I think I share more qualities with my father, my mother's influence is never far away. I share her preference for indoors and the warmth of a bed rather than outdoors and the floor of a tent like my father. Like her, I could never understand why my father would opt to buy an old vehicle and spend large amounts of money keeping it in "good" condition instead of purchasing something new. Yes, I now realize how alike my parents and I really are and how much of their characteristics were passed on to me and have become my characteristics. As I adapted to life in their home, my behavior and beliefs were changed.

As I look at my brother I find that he too is somewhat of an incorporation of various elements from our parents. He has my mother's quiet strength and stamina, choosing to fight his battles in the closet of his own mind rather than sharing them with those around. Like her, he seldom reveals his true feelings on things. He has her love for simplicity of lifestyle, taking pleasure in the small comforts which come from time to time.

My brother and I have both become microcosms of our parent's personalities. Oh they have taken on our own characteristics as they have been shaped by the unique blend of qualities that comprise who we are. But make no mistake, the basic traits are present and their sources become clearly recognizable upon even the slightest effort of investigation. The question as to how these characteristics became a part of our personalities has always puzzled me, especially given that I myself am adopted and do not share my parent's genetic make-up. The answer lies close to the idea of the intimate bond developed between parent and child as the child seeks to adjust to life in this new environment. Somewhere during my formative years, or rather, everywhere during my formative years, I was imbibing the spirit of my parents, embracing and reacting to their strong influences in my life. I am their *real* son, not simply some *legal* heir to their estate, and I have all the character traits to prove it. Through a process of slow transformation, I learned what it meant to love them as my life took on and became a part of their lives.

The relationship between parent and child illustrates how the legal phase must give way to the relational side of adoption. It is in the intimate bond of family–God's family–of which we are now a part by virtue of our adoption, that the qualities and characteristics of God's own nature are passed to us. Within the dynamic of familial give and take, we discover that we begin to develop habits reflective of God's actions. This suggests not only that we receive characteristics from Jesus as the head of the family but also from the church, that is, the community constituting the family itself.

My illustration, like all illustrations, breaks down at certain points. God is not an imperfect parent, meaning that our reaction against God's character involves our own rebellion more than establishing a unique identity. In fact, establishing our identity actually happens when we strive to plunge ourselves deeper in relationship with God. He wants us to become his *real* sons and daughters by conforming our own lives to him and so taking on his life. Our becoming like God in our holiness is analogous to our being like our parents in our personality. My sharing characteristics with my father does not mean that I am my father. We still remain distinct persons, unique bundles of traits and characteristics. Likewise, as I take on God's holy character, I do not become God, or even a god, although I do inherit God's own traits.

Ultimately, we are all orphans whom God has adopted out of the world. In adopting us, God is liberating us from the numerous forms of slavery that the disease of sin brings. We are initially adopted through the work of Christ and the reception of the Spirit in our lives by which we learn what it means to call God our Father. However, as we have seen, this is the first step in a new journey whereby we must *adjust* to a new family life. As members of God's new family, God wants us to move beyond mere *legal* heirs to his kingdom and become his *real* sons and daughters. In fact, salvation is about God making us real sons and daughters, which requires our complete transformation to the new way of living. It is only at the end of the process that we will become fully conformed to Christ and so enter into the full reality of our adoption as sons and daughters. We are adopted and yet fully forming our adoption. As Paul says, "we who have the first fruits of the Spirit even we ourselves groan within ourselves, eagerly waiting for the adoption, the redemption of our body" (Romans 8:23; *NKJV*). Salvation is both our initial adoption into the family of God and our fully realizing that adoption over time as we are transformed. When God invites us to be a part of his family, he wants to make us his *real* children who take on his traits and show them to the world.

Sanctification, Conversion and Discipleship

To say that God wants to make us real sons and daughters is simply another way of stating that God is interested in making disciples. As anyone knows, discipleship is a lengthy process by which an individual conforms her life to Christ. In fact, one could use the term disciple to describe the entirety of the Christian life. Christians are those who attempt to follow Christ in all that they say and do. They are disciples undergoing discipleship with the master.

One way of thinking about discipleship is in terms of being an apprentice serving under a master craftsman. An apprentice seeks to learn a particular way of doing things from a master. The master is the person who has reached the peak of his craft. He has become so good at what he does that he needs no more training. In a sense, a master has reached his complete potential. When a person enters into an apprenticeship, she must learn a new way of doing things and unlearn old patterns of behavior. Slowly as she implements what her master teaches her, she is transformed into a master herself such that she can begin to teach others.

Consider the great Renaissance painter Leonardo da Vinci (d. 1519), who is best known for his famous painting the Last Supper. It would be fair to say that, in many respects, da Vinci had completely developed his talents or potential as a painter. Now, imagine becoming an apprentice of da Vinci's where you were learning how to paint from the hands of this master. Da Vinci might say to you that skill at painting is only a part of becoming a great painter. You must also change the way you look at the world. He might ask you,

> Tell me when you look at that those trees, what do you see? Do you see the colors of the leaves? The way the reds and yellows and browns all blend together to form a rich hue? Do you see the rich textures in the bark? How in some places the bark is peeling and rough while in other places it is smooth? Do you see? Do you *really* see the trees in all of their glory? To be a painter you must learn to see the colors and textures of the world with clarity!

To enter an apprenticeship with da Vinci would mean learning the skill of moving a brush on a canvas *and* learning the skill of seeing all of the shapes, colors and textures of the world. It would necessitate the ability to read the lines on the face of an old man–how they reveal the man's deep wisdom and experience of life–and then be able to paint the same characteristics on a canvas. All of this and more would be required to learn how to be a true painter. As with any other apprentice, the amateur painter would have to unlearn one way of viewing the world and learn a new way of looking at it. She would become a master only after she learned from da Vinci how to see the world and capture that same world on the painter's canvas. This captures the heart of discipleship. It is about learning a new way of looking at the world and a new way of doing things.

When we think of discipleship as being an apprentice, we can see that it is really about conversion from one way of life to another. Many Christians tend to view discipleship as what happens after conversion. They see conversion as the starting point for the Christian walk that must be followed by the hard work of becoming a disciple. When Christians talk about being "saved" or "born again" they usually have their initial conversion in mind. Some evangelistic methods have reinforced this understanding of conversion. Although approaches to evangelism are slowly changing, many Christians still consider evangelism as getting someone to convert by praying a prayer. This understanding of evangelism tends to equate salvation with the initial step of faith, and so conversion is reduced to that first step. By viewing conversion in this way, we miss its connection to discipleship. Disciples are those who are undergoing continuous conversion and true converts are those engaged in discipleship. It's not a movement from one to the other as though conversion and discipleship represent different stages of the Christian life. As Gordon Fee forcefully states, "Too long the church has understood 'conversion' as having only to do with the beginning point. Biblically understood, conversion has to do with making *disciples* of former pagans like ourselves (even if we were born into Christian homes, we need to be 'converted' in this sense). Our Lord did not say, 'Go and make converts' but 'Go and make disciples.' In the long run, only disciples are converts."[3] The Christian life is a life of conversion and a life of discipleship.

One of the best places to see the connection between conversion and discipleship is the Sermon on the Mount (Matthew 5-7). In those brief three chapters, Jesus calls his disciples to convert themselves over to a new way of living in the world. It is no mistake that Dietrich Bonhoeffer, a Lutheran pastor and theologian, structured his book *The Cost of Discipleship* around Matthew 5-7. The Sermon on the Mount provided Bonhoeffer with an opportunity to reexamine the nature of salvation from the perspective of Jesus' call to discipleship. For Bonhoeffer, the call to discipleship issued in the Sermon is one of costly grace not what he called "cheap grace." As he states, "Cheap grace is grace without discipleship, grace without the cross, grace without Jesus Christ, living and incarnate."[4] Over against this Bonhoeffer suggests that costly grace "is the gospel which must be *sought*

---

3. Gordon Fee, *Paul, the Spirit and the People of God* (Peabody, MA: Hendrickson, 1996), 75.

4. D. Bonhoeffer, *The Cost of Discipleship*, second edition, trans. R. H. Fuller (New York, NY: Macmillan Publishing, 1959), 47.

again and again, the gift which must be *asked* for, the door at which a man must *knock*. Such grace is *costly* because it calls us to follow, and it is *grace* because it calls us to follow *Jesus Christ*. It is costly because it costs a man his life, and it is grace because it gives a man the only true life."[5] The entirety of salvation can be reduced to Jesus' one request, "Come, follow me." This request is a call to enter into a new life of discipleship that demands transformation from the person.

Bonhoeffer goes on to suggest that the call to discipleship is a call to single-minded obedience. Any close examination of the nature of Christian discipleship makes it clear that only a complete transformation through exclusive obedience to Christ will due. There can be no separation between faith and obedience as though one precedes the other. "For faith is only real when there is obedience, never without it, and faith only becomes faith in the act of obedience."[6] In James' words, a faith that does not issue forth in true acts of obedience has no life in it (Jas. 2:14-26). So radical is Christ's call that there is little room left for innocent bystanders. It is a call to get in, get out or get run over. As Bonhoeffer, who himself was put to death by the Nazi's in 1945, puts it, "When Christ calls a man, he bids him come and die." This is true conversion plain and simple. It is a life time of dying to oneself and converting over and over to Christ. We cannot begin to consider the nature of Christian discipleship without immediately thinking of a single-minded obedience that brings about a total change.

If we are not careful all of this talk about discipleship and conversion may cause us to lose sight of Christ's ultimate aim.

---

5. Ibid.
6. Ibid., 69.

Entering into an apprenticeship with Christ is not like engaging in any apprenticeship. Christ is not a mere human being. He is the eternal Son of God. When Christ bids a man to come a die, he also bids a man to come and live, really live. This is the puzzle of Christianity. By dying, we live and we live only when we die. What I mean is that disciples of Christ are being transformed into the glorious likeness of the eternal Son of God. They are being healed of the disease of sin, which leads to death, and are coming to possess the abundant life only available through Christ. To be completely cured of this disease requires a kind of death to a way of living in the world that is self-destructive and an open embrace to a new way of living that will ultimately lead to life. We must never forget that Christ's call to come and die is *really* a call to come and live. It is just that to live we must die to patterns of behavior and ways of thinking that bring about our own spiritual demise.

Having now examined adoption and discipleship in terms of conversion to a new way of life, it should begin to become clear why sanctification stands at the center of salvation. Sanctification is certainly about separation from the world, but God separates us by a slow and steady transformation. When I say separation from the world, I mean a separation from self-destructive patterns of thinking and behaving. Following the Gospel and letters of John, we could call these patterns of behavior *worldly* as long as we remember that *worldly* refers to behavior that emerges from life without God (see 1 John 2:15-17). As I mentioned in the first chapter, this is what results from the disease of sin. Entire communities can be given over to *worldly* behavior like racist attitudes and actions that devalue other human beings. We should also not forget that we are all *worldly* to the extent that we all engage in self-destructive behavior that blinds us to the truth. God wants to separate us or sanctify us from those behaviors because God knows that they will destroy us in the end.

God's sanctifying transformation of our lives, i.e., the demand for holiness, is really for our good. God is not simply interested in making us jump through hoops for the sake of watching us jump. No master makes his apprentice do things that are frivolous even if they sometimes may seem that way. A true master knows that everything he makes his apprentice do is ultimately for the good of the apprentice. It is to help the apprentice develop her complete potential. In 1984 a movie came out called the Karate Kid. It was about Daniel, a kid who learned karate from the hands of a Japanese handyman named Mr. Miyagi. At one point in his training, Mr. Miyagi asked Daniel to wax about six cars in his yard using a particular method. Daniel had to put on the wax by moving his left hand counterclockwise and take off the wax by moving his right hand clockwise.

Initially, Daniel did not question Mr. Miyagi because he wanted to please his master. However, by the end of the day he decided that he was finished with this pointless task. He stormed over to Mr. Miyagi and demanded to know why he was waxing cars instead of learning karate. Instead of giving him a direct answer, Mr. Miyagi began throwing punches directly at Daniel. To Daniel's surprise he immediately starting deflecting the punches by moving his left hand counterclockwise and his right hand clockwise, the exact motions he had been using to wax the cars. What Daniel thought initially was a frivolous activity turned out to be designed to develop his skill at karate. God does not ask us to live holy lives just because he wants to watch us put on and take off certain behaviors. God knows that his call to transform our lives is a healing call that helps us grow and develop so that we can reach our full potential.

Holiness, Beauty and Perfection

Up to this point, I have discussed how sanctification relates to our becoming complete disciples of Christ through a process of conversion. The process of conversion itself is the way God heals us, a point I will develop further in chapter six. While conversion is a lengthy process involving our transformation, it remains dependent upon the divine medicine of Christ and the Spirit. The medicine that comes to us is nothing less than God's own life and power being poured into our lives. God *sent forth* his Son and Spirit into the world to heal and deliver. Through our adoption into his family, God himself has become the cure. As we "convert" our lives, we receive God's life and take on his character because we are gradually conformed to the eternal Son of God through the eternal Spirit of God. It is a life of holiness and happiness. This is the other side of sanctification. It is not simply a separation from self-destructive lifestyles, but a union with God's own life such that we come to reflect that life in all that we do. God desires to bring us into a condition where we reflect all that he is, a being whose existence must be described as the beauty of perfection. What we need to begin to see is the connection between holiness, beauty and happiness. God's holiness is his beauty and this beauty gives rise to his happiness. It is my hope that by helping us to see holiness as the beauty of perfection, we will begin to glimpse what it is that God has for us. We are being transformed from those deformed by the disease of sin to those made beautiful by the grace of God.

In his theology of the Old Testament, Walter Brueggemann discusses the relationship between beauty and holiness.[7] He first points out the connection between the tabernacle as a place of beauty *and* a place set apart for God. It is clear from the description of the tabernacle offered in Exodus 25-31 that it was to be a place of unsurpassed glory and splendor precisely because it was the place where God's own glory and splendor would dwell. The gold, the precious stones, the lavish fabrics, the artistic design all pointed toward the magnificence and loveliness of God. This is the pattern that God himself gave to Israel (Ex. 25:8-9). As Brueggemann suggests, this pattern is also reflected in Solomon's construction of the temple (1 Kings 6:14ff). Solomon spares no expense in building an elaborate structure and furnishing it with the finest woods and metals. And, once again, God's glory comes to dwell in this glorious house (1 Kings 8:10). The design of the tabernacle and the temple tell us something about the nature of holiness. Holiness is not simply being set apart but also concerns *how* we are set apart. Most people focus on being set apart while losing sight of the fact that how God sets us apart is by calling us to reflect his own beauty in the world. The tabernacle is set apart as a place

7. Walter Brueggemann, *Theology of the Old Testament: Testimony, Dispute, Advocacy* (Minneapolis, MN: Fortress Press, 1997), 425-29.

of beauty; its beauty reflects God's beauty; its splendor, God's splendor.

God's use of material objects for the tabernacle and temple should not cause us to dwell on the objects themselves. It would be a misreading of these texts to think that they imply we must begin to clothe ourselves with fine apparel and jewelry as the best way to demonstrate God's holiness. The gold and precious stones reflect what the Psalmist would later describe as "the beauty of holiness" (Ps. 29:2; 96:9). When he placed the ark in the tabernacle at Jerusalem, David himself proclaimed to all Israelites that they should "worship the Lord in the beauty of holiness" (1 Chron. 16:29). Brueggemann suggests that the phrase "beauty of holiness" prompts us to see the presence of the Lord as involving a holiness that reflects "symmetry, proportion, order, extravagance, awe, and overwhelmingness."[8] That is, God's holiness is to be found in the beauty arising from the order and harmony at the center of his life. It is the beauty of God's own perfect goodness where nothing is out of place, but all of God's actions and thoughts blend together in perfect harmony and move as one in the same righteous direction. This is the one true harmony of Father, Son and Holy Spirit and it is to be reflected in the harmony and wholeness (*shalom*) God desires for the world.

Consider for a moment what the disease of sin does to humans. It disfigures and deforms lives. This happens through the breakdown of relationships on multiple levels. As an inborn and self-inflicted disease, sin is about the breakdown in the harmony and order within us. We are

---

8. Ibid., 427.

constantly engaged in an interior battle where our natural desires and our acquired desires work against one another. We make self-destructive choices that disfigure our lives and lead down dead-end paths culminating in our own death. As a socially inflicted disease, sin is about the breakdown in the harmony and order within the human family. We do not live at peace with one another or with our environment. Instead, we constantly hurt and wound our fellow human beings with our words and deeds. We also constantly destroy our planet, consuming its resources. Finally, the disease of sin drives a wedge between us and God. Like a savage addiction to some drug pits a child against his parents, sin rips apart our connection to God. In all of these ways, sin disfigures the beauty of God's creation by destroying its harmony and order.

Holiness and sanctification are about the restoration of harmony and order where all that we do reflects the perfect goodness of God. To say that God wants to sanctify us is to say that God wants our lives to display the order and harmony of his life. When we reflect the order and harmony at the center of God's own life, we will be separated from all *worldly* kinds of behavior. This is *how* he sets us apart. Like the tabernacle and the temple, our lives become places where his glory dwells as they slowly take on the beauty of his perfection.

How can our lives reflect God's beauty? What does it mean to display God's own harmony and order? To understand my point better, we need to think about what it means for people to take on a kind of beauty when they are engaged in some activity. Some people do what they do so well that we can see in their performance a kind of beauty. We have a phrase that we use to describe the beauty of some activity, "poetry in motion." Have you ever watched someone play a sport so well that you described it as "poetry in motion?" What about a musical performance? Have you watched a pianist play so well that you thought it was "poetry in motion?" What do we mean when we claim to have seen "poetry in motion?" We usually have in mind the beauty of the performance. Poetry itself has a kind of orderly and harmonious pattern to it that we can detect in its rhymes and rhythms. When we describe a performance as poetry in motion, whether it be playing a sport, a musical instrument or something else, we are referring to the order and harmony in the actions. Poetry in motion is the perfect blend of actions where all parts work together to produce a whole that is greater than the sum total of the parts themselves.

Consider the example of a baseball pitcher like Sandy Koufax. When I was younger I had the privilege of getting Sandy Koufax's autograph at the spring training camp of the Los Angeles Dodgers in Vero Beach, Florida. It was a moment I will never forget because, to put it bluntly, Sandy Koufax is one of the greatest pitchers to ever play the game of baseball. One of the greatest moments of Koufax's career was on September 9, 1965, when he pitched the perfect game. In baseball, a no-hitter where a pitcher does not allow any hits is remarkable enough. However, a pitcher could have a no-hitter and still not pitch a perfect game. He could throw enough balls to walk someone. A perfect game is one of those rare occasions where a pitcher essentially makes no mistakes. In her review of *Sandy Koufax: A Lefty's Legacy* by Jane Leavy,

Teresa DiFalco provides an apt description: "A perfect game occurs when a pitcher throws nine complete innings with no hits, walks, errors, or base runners. Twenty-seven men walk up to the plate, and twenty-seven men sit down. It may be the most phenomenal athletic feat in all of sports, requiring amazing physical and mental stamina. It is riveting to watch."[9] The performance is described as perfect because it represents the best a pitcher can do. On September 9, Sandy Koufax had reached his complete potential as a pitcher; he pitched the perfect game.

There are other details about Koufax's performance that night which make it even more amazing. For one, he had arthritis in his pitching elbow and was planning on retiring because the pain was so intense. The entire time Koufax was pitching a game free from mistakes, he was in excruciating pain. Secondly, almost by accident, a three-minute film segment of Koufax's pitching was made. The film was shot by a trainer because the Dodger coaches wanted to see Koufax's pitching motion in order to help him. Since the trainer only had three minutes of film he decided just to tape Koufax's pitches. What appears on the film is Sandy Koufax throwing pitch after pitch. When she was being interviewed by Terrence Smith on The MacNeil/Lehrer NewsHour, Jane Leavy noted that the film revealed how each pitching motion repeated the one before.[10] According to Leavy, it was this

9. Teresa DiFalco, review of *Sandy Koufax: A Lefty's Legacy*, by Jane Leavy, PopMatters Online.
<http://www.popmatters.com/books/reviews/s/sandy-koufax.shtml> Retrieved 16 February 2004.
10. Jane Leavy, "Conversation: Lefty's Legacy," interview by Terence Smith, *The NewsHour* October 21, 2002.

action that made Koufax perfect that night. With every pitch, he was able to repeat the same fluid motion. Koufax struck out fourteen batters during the course of the game, which means that he had the same fluid motion at least forty-two times. His performance was nothing less than poetry in motion because each wind-up and pitch involved a rhythmic movement that delivered strike after strike after strike.

Sports players like Koufax are given heroic status because they perform feats that are rare among humans. This is why we single them out. They attain a kind of beauty and perfection in their sport that others cannot duplicate. We could say that on one September evening Sandy Koufax achieved the beauty of perfection as a baseball pitcher. His performance reached such a level of play that it far surpassed normal performance even among professional baseball pitchers. By looking closely at Koufax's performance we can gain a glimpse of the beauty of perfection God wants us to reflect in our lives.

First, *we will reflect God's beauty of perfection when we are able to perform our best.* Koufax pitched the *perfect* game because his performance was the best a pitcher can do. To be sure, he did not arrive at a state of absolute perfection, which only God can possess. The perfection we will come to possess is really better described a reaching our complete potential. Koufax had reached his potential as a pitcher. He could go no higher. When we reach our potential as *human beings* created in God's image, we will enter a kind of perfection. At that point, we will truly be doing the best we can do. Let me put it

<http://www.pbs.org/newshour/conversation/July-dec02/leavy_10-21.html>
Retrieved 17 February 2004.

this way, when the image of God is fully developed in us such that we *really* do reflect God's life, then we will be complete or perfect. This is the kind of perfection God wants us to have. It is a *reflection* of his absolute perfection because we are doing the best *we* can do not the best *God* can do.

Second, *we will reflect God's beauty of perfection when our mind, will and body are working together in order and harmony.* The perfection of Koufax's performance resulted from his ability to focus himself toward reaching one goal: throwing strikes across the plate. There was nothing out of sync that night; no wayward thought leading him astray; no desire pushing him in another direction. Instead, he was able to point all of his desires in the same direction. The order and harmony of his performance resulted from the way he organized all of his thoughts and desires. For a brief period of time, they were not working against one another, but all were working together. In pitching terms, he made no "unrighteous" choice because every choice was an example of the *right* way to deliver a baseball to the batter's plate.

Third, *we will reflect God's beauty of perfection when we arrive at true integrity.* None of us have integrity. Why? Because true integrity comes from wholeness and none of us are whole yet. The term integrity means full, whole or complete. When we talk about someone having integrity we usually mean that their actions are consistent with what they believe. In other words, their beliefs and behaviors are functioning together as a harmonious whole. Their actions reflect the moral demands they believe God has made of them. Sandy Koufax certainly achieved a kind of integrity the night he pitched. He experienced what it was like to function as a *whole* where thoughts, desires and choices all worked as one. His pitching aligned itself with his beliefs about the right way to pitch. God always functions as a whole. He never has a wayward thought or desire whereas we always have wayward thoughts and desires. We will possess integrity, when, by God's help, we *integrate* all the various parts of our lives so that they function as a whole. Complete integrity emerges from complete transformation where every part of us is working together as one.

Fourth, *separation from the world happens as we slowly come to reflect God's beauty of perfection.* Do you think that anyone watching Sandy Koufax thought of him as just another pitcher? The beauty of Koufax's performance that night separated him from almost all other professional baseball pitchers. Today his plaque hangs in the baseball hall of fame because he was separate or different and everyone who knows baseball knows it. This is how God separates Christians from the world. For Christians, it's not about the beauty of pitching. It's about the beauty of a life where everything is functioning as it should, as God intended it to function. What we are striving toward is a kind of order and harmony among our thoughts and desires such that we always choose what is right before God. The closer we come to that kind of performance in our lives, the more we take on God's own moral and spiritual beauty. When that kind of performance is on display, it automatically separates us from the world. While sanctification is about separation from the world, we cannot forget that this separation is a natural result of our reflecting the beauty of God's own life. We need not worry about maintaining some sort of conscious distance from everything and everyone. Like Koufax, as we come to reflect the beauty of perfection everyone will take notice. We will be in the world but not of the world.

Finally, *we will reflect God's beauty of perfection when we are fully healed*. Koufax's performance on that night came at the end of a long struggle of learning how to control his behavior and focus his mind. When Koufax first entered professional baseball, he could not control his pitches. He threw the ball fast, but he was also wild. He could not consistently throw strikes and so was ineffective as a pitcher. Through constant practice, he had to transform himself from a wild pitcher to one who could consistently throw strikes. He had to remove the defects in his pitching before he could achieve perfection. God has to remove all of our defects before we fully reflect the beauty of his perfection. Sanctification concerns the gradual removal of the disease of sin through the work of Christ and the Spirit so that one day this corruptible shall put on incorruption and this morality shall put on immortality. When the disease is finally removed in its entirety, then we will be perfect.

What is the purpose of sanctification or holiness? Is holiness just about demonstrating loyalty to God or is it more about a real transformation? I hope by now you can see that I believe it is about the latter. God wants to transform us so that we can reflect the beauty of his perfection in our lives. When God adopts us into his family, he invites us to enter into a new way of living that is good for us. He wants *real* sons and daughters who love him and long to be like him. Likewise, the radical call to discipleship is really a radical call to be all that God has created us to be. When Jesus bids a man to come and die, he is really saying, "Come to me and *live*." We truly come to live when we reflect the beauty of God's own perfection in our lives. When we arrive at the place where our thoughts and desires no longer work against us, but as one push us in the right direction. No doubt, what I am describing requires a long and hard journey. What we must keep in mind is that this is a healing journey whereby we are slowly separated from the self-destructive patterns of behavior that now dominate "the world." God's call is to be transformed; to be healed; to be human.

Chapter 4
The Call to be Human

Do not be ashamed, then, of the testimony about our Lord, or of me his prisoner,
but join with me in suffering for the gospel, relying on the power of God,
who saved us and called us with a holy calling, not according to our works
but according to his own purpose and grace.
This grace was given to us in Christ Jesus before the age began, but it has now
been revealed through the appearing of our Savior Jesus Christ, who
abolished death and brought life and immortality to light through the gospel.
(2 Timothy 1:8-10; NRSV)

Most of the time when Christians discuss the nature and purpose of God's call they focus on the specific call that God has for each person. This idea of calling may be better explained by the word vocation because vocation points to a particular arena in and through which a person "works" for God. Sometimes our vocation can be the same as our career choice, but this is not always the case. Teachers provide good examples of those whose career and vocation go hand in hand. Yet, there are many persons who pursue a career in business in order to provide for themselves and their families while also pursuing their vocation. Someone who feels called to minister to the homeless in the inner city may also work at a bank as an occupation. The former is her vocation and the latter her career. When we ask the question, "What has God called me to do?," we normally associate it with the specific vocation God wants us to pursue.

While this idea of calling is important, we also need to consider the general call God has for all human beings. I'll identify this general call to all human beings as the calling to fellowship. Examining calling from this perspective broadens it from the specific arena to which God calls us as individuals to God's purpose for us as members of the human race. We should keep in mind that calling always relates to God's purpose for our lives. God's specific vocation refers to his purpose for each individual that directly relates to their sharing as co-workers in his mission of reconciling and restoring the entire world. This specific calling may be termed God's calling to witness.[1] At the same time, God has a purpose for all humans that pertains to their being the recipients of his work of reconciliation and restoration and not just co-workers.

Let's think about this for a moment. God's specific call to pulpit ministry, ministry to the homeless, ministry in a foreign land, etc., is how individuals share in God's mission or evangelistic endeavors through Christ and the Spirit to reconcile and restore the entire world. This is the calling to witness. In this sense, Christians become God's agents of reconciliation (cf. 2 Cor. 5.16-21). However, Christians are also

---

1. I take the phrases calling as a matter of fellowship and calling as a matter of witness from George Hunsinger. See his *How to Read Karl Barth: The Shape of His Theology* (New York, NY: Oxford University Press, 1991), 173-83.

those who are being reconciled and restored at the same time that they serve as agents of reconciliation. The restoration of the relationship between God and the individual remains an ongoing process. This is the calling to fellowship. When considering God's general call to all humans, we should think of it as God's call to fulfill one's purpose as a human being, which God brings about by gradually restoring humans to full relationship with himself.

Calling to Fellowship (General Call)	Calling to Witness (Specific Call)
God's purpose for us as human beings	God's purpose for us as participants in his mission
Recipients of reconciliation	Agents of reconciliation
Those being transformed and change	Agents of God's transforming grace

To come at the same idea from a different angle, let's consider what it means to be created in the image of God. God created humans in his image, which suggests that God has designed humanity with a purpose. Moreover, this purpose reflects a general calling God has issued to be all that God has designed humans to be. Sin may have frustrated God's purpose for humanity, but it was not destroyed. If sanctification is the heart of salvation because it is how God seeks to restore his image in human beings fully, then the call to holiness goes together with the call to be human. Hence, sanctification is the process of being made holy, which restores humans to full fellowship with God and enables them to fulfill God's original purpose of becoming all that he has designed them to be. In other words, only when we complete the process of sanctification and become conformed to Christ do we fully realize our potential as those created in God's image.

God's call to live a holy life is the same as God's call to live a human life. Holiness is God's way of indicating to us the purpose for humanity by showing us the kind of life He intended us to live. When Jesus declares, "the thief does not come except to steal, and to kill, and to destroy. I have come that they may have life, and that they may have it more abundantly" (John 11:10; *NKJV*), he seems to be indicating the kind of life he wants to give us. Abundant life is not just eternal life in the sense that we will live forever, it is also our sharing God's triune life, the life of holiness. God created humans in his image with the original intention of enabling them to share in his life. Second Peter clearly communicates this idea when it indicates that God's divine power enables believers to participate or share in the divine nature (2 Pet. 1:3-4). As I indicated previously, since God is holy *and* happy, sharing God's life means participating in a kind of life that is abundant, holy, and happy. Ultimately, the kind of life in view is the kind of life that flourishes or prospers, that is, reaches its complete potential. When humans reach their complete potential, they come to reflect the beauty of God's own perfect life and experience the abundance of that life. This is the general calling God has for the entire human race.

We must understand that pursuing holiness *is* pursuing abundant life because only then will we find the motivation to make holy choices over the course of our lives. In this chapter, I want to explore the nature and purpose of God's general call to the human race and how it relates to God's specific vocation for us as individuals. I also want to discuss the purpose of the church in this chapter as a part of God's call to live a holy life. Many persons do not take the need to be a part of a church seriously enough because they do not see the connection between being a part of the body of Christ, being conformed to Christ and flourishing as a Christian. How can we become conformed to Christ through a holy life apart from the body of Christ? How can we reach our full potential in Christ (flourish) without the admonition and support of the Christian community? How can we engage in true discipleship without belonging to a group of disciples? As God's new community, the church is vital to fulfilling both our call to live a holy life and our vocation to work for God. We begin to live an abundant life as we become a part of the body of Christ, and in that body we learn how to fulfill God's call to be holy and God's call to work for him in holiness.

The Call to be Human

There is no clear place where God issues his general call to humanity. This call is not trumpeted forth from the halls of heaven in the same way that Isaiah's call to speak to the nation of Israel comes forth from God's throne (Isaiah 6). God's general call does not come with a shout but with a whisper. It is God's hushed whisper into a person's ears that she is ordained for something more. Every human senses it deep within the core of her being. She hears the divine whisper in her dissatisfaction with life. Her restlessness; the unsettled sense that there must be more to her own life. Augustine (d. 430), a theologian from the early church captures this whisper so well when he states, "You arouse man that he may delight in praising you because, O Lord, you have made us for yourself and our hearts are restless until they rest in thee."[2] God arouses us at the center of our lives because, as Augustine puts it, he had made us for himself. The divine whisper is simply, "I have made you for myself."

God's voice is not heard aloud with the ears. It comes from within us. If we listen closely we hear this whisper in our own hearts. "Our hearts are restless," Augustine proclaims. Our desires take us here and there. We yearn and yearn and yearn for the stuff of life but cannot quite find contentment and satisfaction. Oh yes, we have small bites of contentment here and gain some satisfaction there. The problem is, it's never enough. Like tantalizing scraps thrown to the floor, we lick up the delights of this world only to find ourselves more and more hungry. Our desires cannot be satisfied. We are people lost in a foreign land, wandering aimlessly throughout life and searching for some place to rest. We want to go home, wherever that is. And, that's the moment when we hear it. It's no more than a fleeting

---

2. Augustine, *Confessions*, book 1, chapter 1.

impression that there must be more and that your life must have a purpose. It is simply, "I have made you for myself."

When Christians refer to the "God-shaped hole" at the center of the human heart, they are usually drawing out an implication of being created in God's own image. Augustine knows that God has made humanity for himself because humanity is created in the image of God. Moreover, Augustine believes that God's whisper can be found in the image. Many theologians, Augustine included, infer the idea of a general call to humans on the basis of their being created in God's image. From the outset, God has designed humanity to be like him, to reflect his own life and to participate in that life. The restlessness humans experience at times is a direct result of their failure to respond to this general call to be in relationship with God. "Our hearts are restless until they rest in thee."

A brief look at Genesis shows us why theologians associate God's call with the creation of humanity. The text declares, "And God said, 'Let us make man in our image, after our likeness. They shall rule the fish of the sea, the birds of the sky, the cattle, the whole earth, and all the creeping things that creep on earth.' And God created man in His image, in the image of God He created him; male and female He created them" (Gen. 1:26-27; *Tanakh*). The fact that God decides to place the stamp of his own life on humanity suggests that there is a fundamental correspondence between them.[3] It is a

---

3. See H. W. Wolff, *Anthropology of the Old Testament*, trans. Margaret Kohl (Philadelphia, PA: Fortress Press, 1974), 159.

part of God's design that humans be in relationship with him. We could say that from the beginning humanity was created with a bent toward heaven, an openness toward the Creator who fashioned them.[4] Humanity is the one place in all creation where God can see himself. Humans were and are to be the mirror of God's own life.

How is it that humanity mirrors or images God? In the past, some theologians have attempted to locate the image of God in some part of humans. They have suggested that humans mirror God because they can reason with their minds. Since no other animal in creation has the capacity to think in the way humans do, theologians supposed that this must be the way humans reflect God. While the capacity to think may be one part of the way humans reflect God, a close look at the Genesis text suggests that the image cannot be found in a specific place. We should not try to dissect humans in order to discover what exact part makes them like God. Humans simply are the image of God. To be human is to be in the image and to be in the image is to be human.[5] In other words, the image of God is not located somewhere in a person. Instead, it is the whole person and everything about the person. It's like trying to say that what makes a car a car is its engine when, in point of fact, there is so much more to a car than an engine. An engine is only one part of a car. What makes humanity the image of God is not one part, but the sum

4. Ibid., 160; See also C. Westermann, *Genesis 1-11: A Commentary*, trans. John J. Scullion (Minneapolis, MN: Augsburg/Fortress Press, 1984), 157-58.
5. Ibid., 157.

total of all the parts. It is important to get this point because it tells us that the call to be human is a call to be God's image and reflect God's life in our lives. We cannot be all that God intended us to be, we cannot be the human he has created, unless we reflect his life in every area of our lives.

What is it about the whole of humanity that makes them the image of God? In a sense, we have already answered this question. God has designed humanity for relationship–relationship with himself, with one another and with creation. Our mind, will, desires, emotions, etc., all help foster and sustain these relationships. Notice that the Genesis text places the image of God in male/female relations. "In the image of God He created him; male and female he created them." It is as humans exist in relationships that they most fully reflect God and God's own life. Consequently, the image of God has to do with humans developing their inherent capacity for relationship. God has not only created humans for himself, but for one another. While humans were designed for relationship, they must go on to develop those relationships. Even in the garden of Eden, Adam and Eve had to develop and grow in their relationship with God and in their relationship with one another. We make a mistake when we think that Adam and Eve already had everything. What they had was the potential for everything. They had the potential to cultivate their relationship with God and, as they communed with God, they were developing this potential. They were, we could say, learning what it means to be in relationship with God, with one another and with creation. They were learning what it means to be human.

By suggesting that Adam and Eve did not have everything, I am not trying to imply that they were flawed. God did not create them with something wrong. As the old saying goes, "God don't make no junk!" Humans were created good. To say that humans were created good is not the same thing as saying that they were created with everything. It is simply to say that humans were created without any flaws (no sin). There was no obstacle hindering Adam and Eve from pursuing their relationship with God and with one another. However, they did have to pursue these relationships. Moreover, this implies that they had to grow and develop in these relationships. God designed them *for* relationship, but they still had to actively pursue their relationships. When we consider that they still had to do something to cultivate their relationship with God, we can see the point of the command not to eat of the tree. God is not testing their loyalty. Instead, God is calling them to grow in their relationship with him by trusting him even if, at that time, they could not see the entire point of trusting him. Relationships can grow and flourish only in an environment of trust because we don't know everything about another person. To this day, my wife and I must trust each another because, even after eleven years of marriage, we are still learning new things about one another. Our relationship develops and matures through our mutual trust, which forms the basis for that relationship. If we did not trust one another, we could not learn to love one another. Adam and Eve did not have any obstacle keeping them from developing their relationships with God and one another, but they still had to develop them, which means they had to grow and mature.

We should also notice that their growth and development had a purpose. Notice that after they sinned, God banished them from the garden of Eden "lest [man] reach out his hand and take also from the tree of life, and eat, and live forever" (Gen. 3:22; *NRSV*). The fact that God placed the tree of life in the garden tells us that the plan was to bring humans from mortality to immortality. Moreover, we could suggest that this plan was to be the culmination of Adam and Eve's own relationship with God. In and through their relationship with God and with one another, they were growing and developing to the point where one day they would eat of the tree of life and so fully enter into God's own life. It is no mistake that the book of Revelation places the tree of life in the center of the New Jerusalem (Rev. 22:2). God's plan has always been the same. God calls humans to realize their complete potential through their relationship with him. The ultimate purpose of being created in God's image is to share God's own life, which the tree of life exemplifies.

A simple glance at the ten commandments reinforces the idea that humans were designed for relationship. As the heart of God's law, the ten commandments provide a summary of the two great commandments: love God and love neighbor (see diagram). What we see in the ten commandments is God's attempt to remind humans that they exist for him (love

God) and for one another (love neighbor). When sin entered the world, it broke down these relationships in fundamental ways. Sin corrupts God's original design of having humans reach their complete potential through their relationship with him and with one another. Humans were to flourish as they reflected God's own life in and through their relationships with one another. The ten commandments are nothing more than God's reminder that the way to flourish is by restoring proper relationships.

Ten Commandments

Relationship to God (Loving God)	Relationship to Others (Loving Neighbor)
(1) No other gods (2) No idols (3) Wrongful use of God's name (4) Remember the Sabbath	(5) honor your parents (respect for authority) (6) No murder (respect for life) (7) No adultery (respect for marriage) (8) No theft (respect for property) (9) No false witness (respect for truth) (10) No coveting (respect for friendship)

We can understand why God would design humans for relationship if we consider what it means for God to exist as

Father, Son and Holy Spirit. The Christian view of God is that he exists as a trinity of persons. At the center of God's life, we find a relationship between three divine persons. God exists in relationship. If God is triune and God is love then Father, Son and Holy Spirit all exist in a communion of love with each divine person giving and receiving love. When God creates humans in his image, he calls them to reflect the pattern of his own life. This life is abundant because it is filled with the joy and happiness bursting forth in and through the giving and receiving of love by Father, Son and Holy Spirit. Remember I said that the beauty of God's own life can be found in the one true harmony of Father, Son and Holy Spirit. God is absolute perfection *because* God exists in triune relationship and God calls us to reflect that perfection through our relationships with him and with one another.

Having examined what it means to be created in the image of God, we can begin to glimpse the general call to fellowship. From the outset, God has designed humans to be in relationship with him and to share his life. While God created Adam and Eve without any flaws, he still expected them to pursue and develop their relationship with him and with one another. Indeed, this is how humans were and are to reach their complete potential. As humans learned to love God and one another by developing their relationships, they were slowly realizing what it means to mirror or reflect God's own life. They were becoming all that they could be as those created in the image of God; they were becoming more fully human. The road to fellowship with God is much more

91

difficult now that the disease of sin infects humanity. In fact, it is impossible for humans to develop their complete potential apart from being healed by God. To enable humans to flourish in and through a relationship with him, God must lead humanity on an exodus out of sin and death. God must recreate humanity.

Christ, the Spirit and the New Humanity

It is no mistake that Christ is the image of the invisible God (Col. 1:15) and the savior of humanity at the same time. Who better to bring the image of God in humanity to completion than the one who is the exact imprint of the very being of God (Heb. 1:3)? The life, death and resurrection of Christ as a whole communicate that Christ is the one chosen to lead humanity out of sin and death. When we want to find an example of what it means to be a real human being, one in whom the image of God is seen most clearly, we need look no further than Jesus of Nazareth. He is true humanity in all of its glory.

The New Testament uses a variety of different expressions to indicate that God in Christ is creating a new humanity who will fully reflect all that he is. For the book of Hebrews, Christ is the pioneer or captain of our salvation (2:10; 6:20; 12:2). The way God decided to bring many sons and daughters to glory was "to make the captain of their salvation perfect through sufferings" (Heb. 2:10). Jesus is also the "captain [author] and perfecter of our faith" (Heb. 12:2). Taken together, these two passages suggest that Jesus initiates our salvation by showing us how to perfect our own faith through trusting God entirely in the midst of sufferings.[6] Jesus is our captain also in the sense that he alone opens the way to God and makes our restoration possible. This eternal Son who is the radiance of God's own glory and who bears the stamp of God's essence (Heb. 1:3) is the one sent into the world to lead humanity up out of the darkness of its own condition.

While Hebrews chooses the language of captain or pioneer, Paul prefers to describe Jesus as the second Adam or the first fruits of a new way of life (Rom. 5:12-21; 1 Cor. 15:20-23, 45-49). As John Ziesler notes, when Paul contrasts Adam with Christ he is describing two different ways of being human.[7] Whereas Adam failed and introduced sin and death to the world, Christ succeeded and brought about righteousness and peace. "For as by one man's disobedience many were made sinners, so also by one Man's obedience many will be made righteous" (Rom. 5:19). Moreover, the new exodus Christ brings culminates in the resurrection of our bodies. Once again, Paul employs the contrast between Adam and Christ to make his point. "And so it is written, 'The first man Adam became a living soul.' The last Adam became a life-giving spirit" (1 Cor. 15:45). Drawing on Genesis 2:7 where God is said to have breathed the breath of life into Adam, Paul claims that the resurrection body of Christ is not

---

6. See Harold W. Attridge, *Hebrews*, (Hermeneia: A Critical and Historical Commentary on the Bible) (Philadelphia, PA: Fortress Press, 1989), 356.

7. J. Ziesler, *Pauline Christianity*, revised edition (Oxford: Oxford University Press, 1990), 53.

simply life-receiving but life-giving. In many respects, the resurrection of Christ is equal to the tree of life because it is when believers will move from mortality to immortality (1 Cor. 15:53). Christ is the first fruits of this movement or final transformation. As a result, Paul believes that Christ is the second Adam who is forging a new destiny for the human race, which is really the same destiny God has always had in mind. It is to take humanity on a transforming journey where they slowly come to share more and more of God's own life until, at last, they make the final leap to immortality.

Turning to the Gospel of Luke, we discover that Jesus is the heir to David's throne, the one who will deliver his people from their sins and who will be a light unto the Gentiles (Luke 1:35, 68-79; 2:29-32). The way Luke sees Jesus fulfilling his mission to deliver and restore is through the Holy Spirit. The angel tells Mary that the Spirit will come upon her to conceive the child in her womb (Luke 1:35). Moreover, when Jesus enters the synagogue, he reads, "The Spirit of the LORD is upon me, because he has anointed me to preach the gospel to the poor; he has sent me to heal the brokenhearted, to proclaim liberty to the captives... " (Luke 4:18). The same Spirit who conceived Christ in Mary's womb now anoints Christ to bring liberty to those who are held captive in sin. For Luke, Christ is the true king who will bring about a new people of God no longer bound by sin. Christ accomplishes this mission of creating a new people through the Spirit's work in his life.

Although the New Testament writers use different ideas to describe the work of Christ, they all agree that Christ is in the business of constructing a new race of people. In Christ, God is recreating humanity so that they can now reach their complete potential as those created in God's image. In addition, the Gospel of Luke tells us that Christ constructed this new people of God through the Spirit. The Spirit conceived Christ in Mary and helped Christ to complete his mission. We could say that the Spirit's role in the life of Christ conceiving him in Mary's womb and anointing him for ministry corresponds to the two callings we have. We are reborn through the Spirit as those on the path of healing and gradually being transformed into this new humanity. Likewise, we are those anointed by the Spirit to extend God's invitation to the entire world to be a part of this new humanity. When we examine the relationship between the Spirit and Christ, what we discover is that the Spirit enables believer to live out their calling to reach their complete potential in and through Christ, and to be an ambassador of Christ. The Spirit is the key to understanding the connection between the calling to fellowship and the calling to witness. The way Christ calls and creates a new people is by means of the Spirit's work.

In the previous chapter, I examined the nature of our adoption in Christ by looking at Galatians 4:4-5. Galatians 4 indicates the God *sent forth* his Son and the Spirit of his Son to bring about our adoption. If we read the passage in light of

Gal. 2:20, where Paul declares that I am crucified with Christ and I no longer live, yet not I, but Christ lives in me, we can see how it is that Christ lives in the person. The Spirit is the one who makes Christ present. Moreover, Paul suggests that the Spirit is the one who helps the individual put on Christ or be clothed with Christ. This suggests that the Spirit joins us to Christ so as to reconstruct Christ's own life in us. The new humanity that Christ creates comes about as we are joined to Christ through the Spirit. To become a member of God's family is to become a member of this new humanity.

The life of Christian discipleship is a life in the Spirit because it is the Spirit who reproduces Christ's life, death and resurrection in us. If Christ truly is the one who remakes humanity and leads them on a new exodus out of sin and death so that they can reach their complete potential, then the Spirit is the one who actualizes that exodus in the lives of believers as well as in the church, the new community God is creating. Through the Spirit, we are learning what it means to be created in the image of God. In the same way that the Spirit reproduces Christ's life in us, the Spirit distributes Christ's gifts to us. By distributing these gifts, the Spirit is anointing us to be ambassadors extending God's message of salvation to the entire world. This is the calling to witness to the world what God is doing in Christ and in us. The Spirit helps us to fulfill both the calling to fellowship and the calling to witness because the Spirit joins us to Christ and so makes us his disciples.

The Church and Our Twin Vocations

If discipleship helps us to see *how* we live out our twin callings, then the church helps us discover *where* we live out our twin callings. This is because the church is the community of Christ's disciples. It is difficult to discuss the calling of God to discipleship without reference to the people of God. Although some Christians may want to live an isolated Christian life, cut off from their fellow believers, this is not what true Christianity is all about. One cannot be a follower of Christ and not participate in the body of Christ. This means that there is no solitary existence for the Christian. Instead, there is only, as Ray Stedman put it, "body life."[8]

All Christians are "called" to body life because God's salvific work primarily involves establishing a new community who will be his people. I say "called" but in point of fact there is little distinction between putting on Christ and belong to the new community Christ has established. Christians are not "called" to be a part of the church as though there is a time when they live their Christian walk apart from it. To be a Christian is to be a part of the church. When speaking of Paul's view of salvation, Gordon Fee is a forceful as he can be: "... salvation is *never thought of simply as a one-on-one relationship with God*. While such a relationship is included, to be sure, to be saved means especially to be joined to the people of God" (his emphasis).[9] It is clear when one reads the New Testament as a whole that the focus of salvation is not

---

8. Ray C. Stedman, *Body Life* (Glendale, CA: Regal Books, 1972).
9. Fee, *God's Empowering Presence*, 846.

individuals as much as it is the creation of a people. There are various phrases used to describe this new people. They are called the household of God (Eph. 2:19), the citizens of heaven (Eph. 2:19; Phil. 3:20), the church (Acts 2:47; Rev. 2-3), the temple of the Spirit with Christ as the chief corner stone (Eph. 2:20-21; 1 Pet. 2:4-8), the body of Christ (Rom. 12:5; 1 Cor. 10:16) and the royal priesthood (1 Pet. 2:9-10), just to mention a few. Anytime we look for a biblical passage that offers a direct command to belong to a local church, we are missing the point. The New Testament simply assumes that each believer is united to the body and as such must participate in body life. Community life is at the heart of Christianity because God will have a people who reflect his own triune life. We are designed to be in relationship with God *and* with one another.

We need only look to the practice of baptism and the Lord's Supper to see how this is the case. Both are *public* events. That is, they are both performed before and with one's fellow Christians. When a believer is baptized, she is declaring to all present not simply that she is a follower of Christ but also that she belongs to Christ's body. Water baptism signals the believer's commitment to be a part of God's new community and the local congregation's commitment to embrace the new believer. In many respects, water baptism implies a covenant between fellow believers to be there for one another and to help one another. It is a public declaration that the story of our lives as individuals will now become a part of the collective story of the congregation before whom we were baptized. Our life story now becomes a strand of rope intertwined with all other believers who are members of our local congregation. As the public testimony of the Spirit's prior work in making one a member of the body of Christ, water baptism compels us to view ourselves as a part of this new community.

The Lord's Supper is no different. While many Christians view the practice of the Lord's Supper as simply a way to call to mind what Christ has done on the cross, we must think of it differently. Of course, I do not deny that the Lord's Supper is a memorial or a time of remembering what Christ has done. However, we should not allow that fact to cloud its significance as a community event. Paul's description of the Lord's Supper in 1 Corinthians tells us that it took place within the context of the church gathered together to share a meal with one another. The problem with the Corinthian's practice of the Lord's Supper was that they were engaged in divisions and backbiting. The divisions seemed to occur along economic lines with the wealthy separating themselves from the poorer members of the congregation. For Paul, when the wealthy separated themselves from the poor, they denied the point of the Lord's Supper which was that "we though many, are one bread and one body; for we all partake of that one bread" (1 Cor. 10:17). To abuse the body of Christ by introducing division is equivalent to abusing Christ, which is why Paul says that some were eating and drinking judgment upon themselves (1 Cor. 11:29-33).[10] Christ is building a new

---

10. See G. Fee, *The First Epistle to the Corinthians*, New International

community of people who truly reflect God's life by living together in peace, and the Lord's Supper is the public event where that unity is announced. We are one body because we eat one bread. When we participate in the Lord's Supper we publicly commit ourselves to be a part of Christ's body. It is simultaneously a renewal of our covenant with God to be his people and a covenant with one another to live as his people in unity and peace.

The calling to fellowship with God and the calling to witness for God must be lived out in and through this new community that God is forming. If the call to fellowship is a call to realize our complete potential as those created in the image of God, it is difficult to see how we can neglect our membership in the *new humanity* that Christ is forming. We realize God's call to be a human being in the new humanity. It is in the church that we learn how to put on Christ by growing and maturing in that relationship. Moreover, when I say that it is in the church, I do not mean a building but the community, the group of people who identify themselves as the disciples of Christ. Too often we say, "let's go to church" as though we're simply driving to a building to hear a speech, sing some songs and then go home. When we go to church we are gathering as a community of disciples. We learn how to put on Christ and so realize our potential in and through a community of believers who pray for us, challenge us, push us, in short, who live and die with us. This is what it means to intertwine the story of one's own life with others. We become

Commentary on the New Testament (Grand Rapids, MI: Eerdmans, 1987), 533-34.

100

transformed in our lives so that we reflect God's own life by learning how to live together as the new community of God.

How do we know what it means to bear one another's burdens if we don't belong to a community where we must practice it? How can we sympathize with the problems that others face when we never take the time to learn about those problems and to pray for them? Praying for the sick, the downtrodden, the struggles that persons face in our local church is a transforming act. It transforms us because it teaches us to care for others as Christ cared for them. It teaches us how to live as we were designed to live; in relationship with God and with one another. I learned what it means to love people through all the difficult periods of life simply by watching how others in my local church responded to one another. As we shared meals, wept with one another, rejoiced over one another's triumphs and experienced life together, we were transformed by God's grace. We learned what it means to be human in relationship with others as we learned what it means to be the new humanity that God has called into existence.

The importance of belonging to the body of Christ is that we are incorporated into a community of disciples who are putting on Christ by learning to love and care for one another "in the power of the Spirit." We should not lose sight of the fact that Paul's letters are addressed to local churches. When Paul says to the church at Ephesus "be imitators of God as dear children. And walk in love as Christ also has loved us... (Eph. 5:1-2), he is not talking about an attitude that Christians should have in general. There is not an expectation that the

Ephesians will learn to love people in the Roman world whom they have not met. Rather, he is telling the Christians who are gathered together in Ephesus as a community that they should love one another. When he tells the church at Rome that the strong should support the weak among them (Rom. 15:1), he is pointing to the local churches in that city. Paul is essentially saying to them, "When you assembly together as a community, the strong among you should help the weak." The ultimate point of this kind of talk is to suggest that believers cannot fulfill their call to be transformed and to put on Christ unless they learn to care for one another. Only when we are face to face with the real-life problems of our fellow Christians do we begin to learn what it means to love and to embrace. And, when we learn to love, we are transformed.

The church is the place where discipleship is lived out and experienced. We become truly human when we learn to live with other humans and walk with them through life. Walking by the Spirit is a way of living that requires the community of faith, which is why Paul follows his admonition with the advice to "bear one another's burdens." Of course, this means that our church structures should exist to facilitate body life. Admittedly, it is easier for smaller and medium-sized churches to promote body life than larger churches. The larger the congregation the more difficult it is to think of it as a community where people invest in one another's lives. However, this does not mean that larger churches cannot promote community. Small groups are one way larger churches have succeeded in reconnecting their members to one another. In the end though, each church must become intentional about promoting an environment where church members become responsible for one another in tangible ways. It is not enough simply to pray for some request uttered from a pulpit. As believers invest in one another's lives, they learn to be true disciples of Christ. Like the early church, present churches must seek to continue in the apostles' *fellowship*, in the breaking of bread and in prayers (Acts 2:42).

When the church becomes a community of disciples where each person invests in the life of that community, it opens the door for it to become the place where the call to witness occurs. After all, God's call to witness involves a recognition on the part of the community that God is at work in a particular way in the life of one person. How can any community say that God is at work in a person's life when their lives are not intertwined with the life of that person? A quick glance at the New Testament suggests that the calling to witness normally comes in the midst of community life. Paul (Saul) and Barnabas are set apart for missionary work to the Gentiles as the church is gathered together for worship (Acts 13:1-3). Moreover, after the Spirit identifies Paul and Barnabas, the church "lays hands" on them to commission them for this task. Years later when Paul describes Timothy's call, he uses the same language. Paul tells Timothy not to neglect the gift in him, "which was given to you by prophecy with the laying on of hands of the eldership" (1 Tim. 4:14;

NKJV). In both cases, the community of disciples is recognizing God's gifts in particular individuals and setting those individuals forth to do the work of the ministry.

We should not lose sight of the fact that the commissioning of God comes through the laying on of hands. The symbol of human touch is powerful. In extending his blessing through human touch, God is actively seeking to promote community life. God is in the business of strengthening relationships among his people not weakening them. When we become channels of God's grace to other people, God is forging a relational link that we cannot overlook. At minimum, this should tell us that human relationships are important to God. In the touch of one person by another, God breaks down dividing walls of hostility like gender and race and shows us that his kingdom will consist of people from every tribe and tongue. Of course, God can work apart from humans, but he chooses to call us to lay hands on one another because he not only wants to connect us to himself but to one another. The calling to fellowship and the calling to witness are bound up with one another. Even the very act of setting forth a person to be a witness for the kingdom helps to promote fellowship with God and fellow believers.

The call to be human is nothing more than God's general call to the entire race to be all that he has designed us to be. It is a call to realize our complete potential in and through fellowship with God. God has made us for himself, that is, he has made us for relationship with him. We need only look to the image of God to recognize this fact. In calling us to relationship with himself, he also calls us to be in relationship with one another. The image of God is most fully seen in the relationships that exist between fellow human beings. This suggests that community life in all of its dimensions–family life, church life–remains bound up in the call to be human. Although sin warps our relationships and becomes an insurmountable obstacle to fully realizing our potential, God is in the business of redeeming a new humanity from sin and death through Christ and the Spirit. We are called to be a part of this new humanity, the church, because it is the place where we live out our discipleship. The church is the place where we learn what it means to love and to be human. It is also the place where we receive our commissioning to be God's ambassadors proclaiming his divine call to fellowship to the entire world. Here is where God's twin calls come full circle. The call to fellowship is complemented by the call to witness. We are witnessing to the work God is doing in us and in the community to which we belong. By means of the gifts the Spirit imparts and the life the Spirit brings, we proclaim that God is calling us both to participate in his life and to share that life with others. This is the good work that God in Christ Jesus has prepared in advance that we may walk in it (Eph. 2:10).

Chapter 5
Eternal Election and the Pursuit of Holiness

Blessed be the God and Father of our Lord Jesus Christ,
who has blessed us in Christ with every spiritual blessing in the heavenly places,
just as he chose us in Christ before the foundation of the world
to be holy and blameless in love.

(Eph. 1:3-4; NRSV)

When I first became a Christian I wanted to study the Bible as much as I could. Like many young Christians, I was curious to discover the answers to a host of questions I had about Christianity. I remember having conversations with my Catholic friends about the differences in what we believed, arguing over whether Christians were eternally secure with Baptist friends, debating with many of my non-Pentecostal friends about the baptism in the Holy Spirit, and a host of other issues. On the whole, these debates and conversations were fairly light, although at the time I thought I was engaging in deep theological discourse about the biggest questions of life.

One line of questioning that emerged amidst my engagement with scripture concerned the relationship between divine election, predestination and human free choice. After I arrived at college as a freshman, I learned how long the issued had been debated by Christians. For Protestants, this issue goes back as far as the origins of Protestantism and came to a head at the beginning of the 1600s when the followers of James Arminius proposed an alternative explanation to the one given by John Calvin. John Calvin had suggested that God actively predestines some to hell and others to heaven, a doctrine known as double predestination. Although Arminius studied in the very college Calvin himself had founded, he rejected Calvin's view. Arminius thought that double predestination could not be true given the scriptural evidence and the idea of God as perfectly good and perfectly loving. Instead, he sought to work out a system of predestination that centered around the idea of the corporate body of Christ. As a result of Arminius' disagreement with Calvin's position, a debate broke out (Calvinism vs. Arminianism) that continues to the present day.

While some may consider the debate over predestination and God's eternal election as puzzling and mostly irrelevant, I have come to think otherwise. Our views on predestination are important at least for two reasons. First, what we believe to a large degree determines how we behave, and that includes what we believe about predestination. Second, our views about predestination inform what we think about God and the way God works in the world, especially in his dealings with humans. This is because the doctrine of predestination falls under God's providence, which concerns how God governs and cares for the creation. If you think God demonstrates his care by predetermining the eternal destiny of humans, then that belief will affect the way you pray and how you pursue a holy life, as well as many other beliefs. Conversely, if you think that God allows humans the freedom to make choices, then that will also affect how you pray, engage in evangelism, and, yes, live a holy life.

What I hope to do in the present chapter is briefly discuss this complex issue with the intent of acting as a guide who knows the terrain somewhat and can help lead persons past some of the obstacles that present themselves. I do not consider the view I am setting forth to be the definitive answer to predestination and eternal election, but I trust that it is *an* answer that will prove beneficial to those engaged in the pursuit of holiness. It is my hope that after working through the issue, the importance of the debate over predestination and its relationship to human freedom will become clear.

Getting Some Ideas Straight

The initial step in our discussion of predestination and election is to be clear about what we are discussing. First, both election and predestination are biblical concepts and, as such, cannot be avoided. The question is not whether I believe *in* predestination, but what do I believe *about* predestination. Paul declares, "for those whom he foreknew he also predestined to be conformed to the image of his Son..." (Rom. 8:29), and then spends Romans 9-11 unpacking what he means by that statement. In the book of Ephesians, the idea of "being destined" or "predestined" occurs several times throughout the first chapter (cf. Eph. 1:4-5, 11). One could even interpret Jesus' statement that "no one can come to me unless it is granted by the Father" (John 6:65) as implying eternal predestination. Although it may be necessary to reject certain views of predestination and election, this is different from rejecting them altogether.

Once we see predestination and election as biblical concepts, we need to become clear about what these terms do and do not mean. Election is a noun from which we get the verb to elect. Both the noun and the verb have to do with choice. In the same way that an individual makes a choice during a political election, when we speak of eternal election we are talking about God's choice. If we understand it correctly, the term predestination further clarifies God's choice by indicating when that choice occurred. Predestination refers to what God determines (chooses) to do, and in fact does, beforehand. In this sense, it is synonymous with the term foreordain. When we put both terms together, they refer to God choosing a plan of action and implementing it prior to choices made by others. In fact, God makes choices in much the same way that we do. God plans ahead or predetermines what he is going to do just as we plan our day ahead of time. Once God formulates a plan of action (what he will do), he carries it out. Thinking about predestination and election as indicating God's plan of action for the universe, including humanity, can help us sort through the issues.

Since both election and predestination refer to God's prior choices, they must also refer primarily to God's will and not God's knowledge. The difference between God's will and God's knowledge is equal to the difference between what God does and what God knows. While this distinction may seem minor, it is important to keep in mind. For example, if God has perfect knowledge of the future, then God already knows who will and will not go to heaven. The fact that God possesses this kind of knowledge does not mean that God wills to send some to heaven and to send others to hell. To say God predestines is to say that God *wills* beforehand that something will happen, not that God *knows* beforehand what will happen.

Most Christians believe God knows the future. In fact, our prayers seem to depend in part upon God knowing the future, our personal future. One of the reasons why we trust God to guide us through life is because we believe that God knows exactly what lies ahead. Consequently, God can know the future perfectly and not determine by his will what will happen. God can know whether the President of the United States will be assassinated in 2050 and not predetermine or will that the President be assassinated. While I cannot go into detail about how God's knowledge of the future relates to future events, there are good reasons to think that God's knowledge of the future does not mean that God causes or wills it to happen. So there is an important difference between what God knows and what God wills. Election and predestination both refer to what God wills to do, that is, they refer to the implementation of God's plan of action for the universe. With these distinctions in mind, I want to examine predestination and election from three perspectives: electing a people, a person and a plan.

Electing a People
The Chosen People of God in the Old Testament

The first place to begin a discussion of predestination and election is with God's choice of Israel as his people. In the Old Testament, election has more to do with God choosing a group of people than specific individuals. The focus of election always centers upon the community or the people of Israel. When the Old Testament refers to God's choice of an individual it is because the person represents or forms a part of a larger group. For example, the story of Abraham's unconditional election by God is really the story of Israel's election (cf. Gen. 12:1-3; 18:18; 22:18). Abraham's story is another way of God saying to Israel, "you are my special treasure above all other nations" (cf. Ex. 19:5; Deut. 7:6-8). It is not the story of some secret election God made of Abraham before the world began. Instead, the focus upon Abraham has to do with the focus upon the group. One could say that the Old Testament describes the election of Israel as the people of God by telling the story of how God worked in the life of Israel's ancestor Abraham. This is why God keeps announcing himself as the God of Abraham, Isaac and Jacob. It is God's way of identifying his choice of Israel as his people.

A second example of the use of individuals to represent a group is the famous text of Malachi 1:2-3 where God says, "Jacob I have loved; But Esau I have hated." It is clear from the context that Jacob represents Israel and Esau represents Edom, a nation that became Israel's enemy (cf. Num. 20:14-20). There is no indication that God chooses the individual

Jacob from all eternity and rejects Esau from all eternity. Instead, this is another way of describing the choice of the nation. God reminds Israel that she is the object of his love and not Edom. In addition, Malachi indicates that not all Israel will be accepted by God. Even though God loves the nation of Israel, individual Israelites may be rejected if they don't straighten up. The problem is that some Israelites fail to worship God properly (1:7, 12), others fail to abstain from marrying foreign wives (2:11) and still others continue to rob God of tithes and offerings (3:8). When Malachi separates the righteous from the wicked, he has in mind two distinct groups of Israelites not Israelites and non-Israelites (3:18).[1] The righteous Israelites are those who fear God, listen to God and meditate on God's name while the wicked are the proud who tempt God by their failure to adhere to God's covenant. Malachi begins with God's love for Israel as a group and then suggests that certain individual Israelites may remove themselves from this group by their actions. Although Malachi 1:2-3 may seem to refer to the individual election of Jacob and Esau, in fact it is another way of focusing upon the nation or the community.

While the Old Testament concept of election focuses God's choice of a group, it also points toward the open-ended nature of this elected group. That is, exactly who belongs to the elect or those chosen by God remains up for grabs. Indeed,

---

1. See Jon L. Berquist, *Judaism in Persia's Shadow: A Social and Historical Approach* (Minneapolis, MN: Fortress Press, 1995), 100-01. Berquist suggests that Malachi identifies an "in-group" of Israelites who are faithful and an "out-group" who are not faithful. It is the "out-group" God rejects.

the prophetic books provide hints that God will extend his election beyond the borders of national Israel. Nowhere is this idea more clearly stated than in Isaiah 19 where Isaiah describes the conversion of Egypt and Assyria. Isaiah declares, "On that day Israel will be the third with Egypt and Assyria, a blessing in the midst of the earth, whom the LORD of hosts has blessed, saying, 'Blessed be Egypt *my* people, and Assyria the work of *my* hands, and Israel *my* heritage" (my emphasis; 19:24-25). According to Isaiah, the chosen people of God will now include Israel's neighbors to the north and the south. Israel still occupies a central place as "a blessing in the midst of the earth," but the chosen people no longer merely include the physical descendants of Abraham.[2] God has opened up the borders of his elected people.

The story of Jonah further attests to an extension of God's people beyond the borders of national Israel. The book opens with God's command that Jonah go to Ninevah, a city in the Assyrian empire, and deliver a message of judgment and salvation. As Douglas Stuart suggests, the central point of the book is to challenge Jonah's national pride by asserting God's freedom to show compassion on whomever he wants.[3] "What right," God asks Jonah, "do you have to be angry?" (Jonah 4:4, 9). It is clear from chapter four that Jonah is upset with God for extending forgiveness and mercy instead of judgment to the Assyrians. Jonah even cites his anger as the reason why he

---

2. Joseph Blenkinsopp, *Isaiah 1-39*, The Anchor Bible, vol. 19 (New York, NY: Doubleday, 2000), 319-20.
3. Douglas Stuart, *Hosea - Jonah*, Word Biblical Commentary 31 (Waco, TX: Word Books, 1987), 435.

ran away from God. God's final response to Jonah is to ask, "Why should I not be concerned about Ninevah?" (4:11). Just because Israel is God's chosen nation, Jonah should not make the mistake of thinking God cannot and will not invite others to follow him and be his part of his people.

Another dimension that should be noticed in the election of Israel as the people of God is that the shape of this people remains highly flexible in terms of its number. God does not set in stone some exact number of those who will belong to his elect people. We can see this idea expressed most clearly in the concept of a remnant. When Elijah despairs that all Israel has forsaken the covenant, God comforts him by appealing to a remnant of those in Israel who have not bowed their knee to Baal (1 Kings 19:18).[4] Not all Israel are faithful Israel. This much already should be clear from Malachi's message. The problem is that although God has chosen the nation of Israel, many Israelites continue to be unfaithful to the covenant. In light of this problem, it becomes increasingly difficult to identify who exactly belongs to the people of God and who does not. While Israel as a whole remains the chosen people of God, individual Israelites move in and out of this group. The idea of a remnant identifies a group within the nation of Israel who remain faithful. There is always a recognition in the Old Testament that Israelites who were unfaithful ceased to be a part of the chosen people of God.[5] Hence it is never fully clear as to who exactly belongs to the

---

4. For further examination of the concept of remnant see H. H. Rowley, *The Biblical Doctrine of Election* (London: Lutterworth Press, 1950), 69-94.
5. Ibid., 69.

elected nation of Israelites. The number of this group keeps shifting in light of the lack of faithfulness by many individual Israelites.

We can see this continuous shift in the elected people of God by looking closely at God's choice of Jeroboam to lead the northern kingdom of Israel (1 Kings 11). Although Solomon is David's heir, toward the end of his reign he displays the same kind of unfaithfulness as other Israelites had done. In light of Solomon's unfaithfulness, God decides to rip the kingdom from the hands of his son and extend his choice to Jeroboam as the one through whom a new kingly dynasty will be formed. God says to Jeroboam, "I will be with you and build for you and enduring house as I did for David" (1 Kings 11:38). This is powerful language. There is no doubt that God is placing his blessing on Jeroboam even to the point that Jeroboam's descendants will remain on the throne forever (an *enduring* house). However, God's choice must be followed by Jeroboam's own faithful response. It does not take long for Jeroboam to act in unfaithful ways with the result that God withdraws his promise (1 Kings 14:6-13). What is so fascinating about this story is how quickly God chooses and rejects Jeroboam. One could say that Jeroboam is elected by God and then abandoned because of his own unfaithfulness. Nevertheless, the northern kingdom of Israel remains. God's rejection of Jeroboam in no way implies that God has rejected Israel as his chosen people. The group remains even while individuals come and go.

We are now in a position to draw some conclusions about the concept of election in the Old Testament. Election

116

primarily concerns a group of people, the nation of Israel. Even God's choice of Abraham must be viewed in terms of the choice of a group of people. This means that election is corporate in nature not individualistic. It may be helpful to think of a corporation like General Motors with lots of employees. Individual employees come and go, but the corporation remains. Likewise, Old Testament writers never clearly define this elect group. Its exact number remains open ended and even other nations are invited to be a part of it. Finally, the ultimate aim of Israel's election is to extend God's message of salvation to the entire world. We find this already in God's promise to Abraham that "in you all the families of the earth will be blessed" (Gen. 12:3). It is also present in the divine call for Israel to be a holy nation of priests (Ex. 19:6) so that she can proclaim God's message to the entire world.

The Chosen People of God in Romans

As a result of our brief survey of election in the Old Testament, we are in a better position to understand Paul's view of election. Anyone who has been in a discussion about election or predestination, knows that eventually Romans is brought up. Romans 9-11, in particular, becomes the place where the debate over predestination is fought. According to one defender of Calvinism, Romans 9 contains the "most significant passage in the New Testament" about predestination.[6] For that reason, we need to get a better grasp of Paul's use of the concept of election in Romans.

---

6. R. C. Sproul, *Chosen By God* (Wheaton, IL: Tyndale House Publishers, 1986), 148.

Throughout our brief discussion, we need to keep in mind the Old Testament concept of corporate election.

Before turning to Romans 9-11, we should keep in mind how those chapters fit into Paul's argument in Romans 1-8. By offering an outline of the first eight chapters, I hope to indicate the larger flow of Paul's thought and how Romans 9-11 represents the logical culmination of his argument. In brief, one could structure Romans 1-8 in the following way:[7]

- Romans 1:1-17: Introduction and main idea (the righteousness of God is revealed in the Gospel of Jesus Christ). It is important to keep in mind that Paul thinks of the righteousness of God in terms of God's faithfulness to the covenant.

- Romans 1:18-3:20: Both Jew and Gentile alike stand under sin (both groups prove to be unfaithful).

- Romans 3:21-4:25: Salvation rests upon the faithfulness of Jesus Christ for all who believe in him in the same way that Abraham believed in God.

---

7. My summary of Romans 1-8 represents a composite picture I have drawn from the work of Gordon Fee, N. T. Wright and Luke Timothy Johnson. See Fee, *God's Empowering Presence*, pp. 472-76; Johnson, *Reading Romans*, viiff; Wright, "New Exodus, New Inheritance: The Narrative Substructure of Romans 3-8" in *Romans and the People of God: Essays in Honor of Gordon D. Fee*, eds. S. K. Soderlund and N. T. Wright (Grand Rapids, MI: Eerdmans, 1999), 26-35.

- Romans 5:1-6:23: God's faithfulness is demonstrated by the faithfulness of Jesus Christ in two ways: (1) Christ's faithful obedience over against Adam's disobedience; (2) Christ's faithfulness in liberating from the Egypt of slavery to sin all those joined to him.

- Romans 7:1-8:39: The problem of unfaithfulness is not a problem of God's law but in the weakness of persons to fulfill it (Rom. 7:1-25). The Spirit corrects the problem of the lack of faithfulness on the part of God's covenant people by enabling them to walk in light of the law and so fulfill the law (Rom. 8:1-39).

My outline of Romans 1-8 suggests that God demonstrates his covenant faithfulness to the chosen people of God in and through Christ's death and resurrection and the Spirit's transforming power. This is the gospel or the good news according to Paul. The power of God unto salvation rests upon God's own faithfulness to liberate from the bondage or slavery of sin the Jew first but also the Gentile through Christ and the Spirit (cf. Rom. 1:16). As the ultimate purpose of Romans 1-8, God's demonstration of his faithfulness in the gospel sets up the immediate expression of anguish Paul gives in Romans 9:1-5 with regard to his own people, the Jews.

If God demonstrates his faithfulness to the covenant with Israel by Christ and the Spirit, then why are so many individual Jews turning away? After all, Israel is the elect people of God and those through whom the promises of God

119

flow (9:4-5). Where do the Jews now fit into the plan of God? The issue surrounding the status of national Israel as the chosen people of God is the logical question that emerges in light of what Paul has said in Romans 1-8. This issue becomes even more apparent given the fact that many Israelites have rejected the gospel. One can see why Paul is in anguish over his own people. Moreover, the rejection of the gospel by many Israelites suggests that maybe God's word has no effect. Can we say that God is still faithful when so many Jewish people do not embrace Christ?

The whole purpose behind Romans 9-11 is to explore the issue of God's faithfulness and Jewish disobedience in light of the election of the nation of Israel. The nation of Israel *is* the chosen (elect) people of God and yet Israelites reject Christ *and* numerous Gentiles accept Christ. To my mind, Paul's answer falls in line with the Old Testament concept of corporate election where God has an elect group of people while individuals move in and out of this group. More specifically, Paul builds upon the idea of a remnant of those faithful to God's promises in order to argue that the chosen people of God has never included all of Abraham's descendants. This is why he begins his argument with, "for not all Israelites truly belong to Israel" (Rom. 9:6-7). In other words, Paul immediately makes the point that not all of Abraham's physical descendants belong to the elect people of God. If we keep this in mind, we can understand why Luke Timothy Johnson forcefully states, "Paul's topic is not the eternal predestination of individual human souls to heaven or hell... Here as throughout the letter, but even more explicitly, Paul conceives of salvation... as a matter of belonging to God's people."[8] To read Romans 9-11 as focusing upon God's electing individuals to heaven or hell is to miss the point of those chapters completely. Their entire purpose is to say that God continues to have a chosen people, a remnant, which includes both faithful Jews and faithful Gentiles.

By examining Paul's argument more closely, we can see how he makes his case that not all of Abraham's physical descendants were a part of God's elect people. Following Malachi, he asserts that both the children of Jacob (the Israelites) and the children of Esau (the Edomites) were physical descendants of Abraham. However, the fact that both groups could claim to be descended from Abraham did not mean that both were a part of God's elect body (cf. Rom. 9:12). It is important to remember that Jacob and Esau represent distinct groups of people and not individuals. The difference between Israel and Edom allows Paul to make a second point that even among the children of Jacob some are faithful and some are not. This is where Paul inserts the idea of a remnant, an idea he gets from the Old Testament prophets (cf. Rom. 9:25-29). There remains a remnant of God's chosen people, which includes all those who are faithful to God. The first step in Paul's argument is to establish that God has a chosen people and that this chosen people has never included all Israelites.

The second step in the argument draws upon the Old Testament idea that God opens up his elect body to include

---

8. Johnson, *Reading Romans*, 140.

the Gentiles. God is in the business of extending the boundaries of his elect people beyond national identity, a point the Old Testament prophets had already made. For Paul, the way God extends those boundaries is through Christ and the Spirit. This is the new work God is doing. How each person, Jew and Gentile, joins himself to this new work of God remains the same: faith. In Romans 9:30-10:15, Paul is at pains to make one point: "that if you confess with your mouth the Lord Jesus and believe in your heart that God has raised him from the dead, you will be saved" (9:9). God's remnant, the elect group of people includes both Jews and Gentiles who express faith in Christ. It is a corporate body open to all who believe.

Some may suggest that you cannot have a corporate concept of election without including individuals. In other words, if God has chosen a group of people, then that group must include individuals. As such, God must predetermine the destiny of individuals in order to predetermine the destiny of a group. It seems to me that this conclusion can only be reached if one ignores how Paul brings his discussion of God's chosen people to a close in Romans 11. He uses an agricultural illustration to reinforce his understanding of how individuals become a part of the chosen people of God (11:16-24). The illustration centers upon an olive tree with branches. The tree itself, which Paul will also refer to as the root (9:18), represents the nation of Israel, the chosen people of God. Paul divides the branches into two types, natural branches and wild branches. The natural branches refer to Israelites and the wild branches refer to Gentile Christians. Paul then clearly indicates that Gentiles (wild branches) who accept Christ are grafted onto the people of God even while Jews (natural branches) who rejected Christ are cut off. However, just as quickly, he suggests that Gentiles themselves who were grafted onto the people of God can be cut off. Consequently, Paul maintains the idea that God has chosen a group of people (the root or the tree) while also stressing that individuals move in and out of this chosen group. There is no secret predestination of one person to heaven or another person to hell here. If we were to ask Paul how someone becomes a part of the people of God he would state, "Because of unbelief they [the natural branches] were broken off and you [the wild branches] stand by faith" (11:20).

At this point I hope it is clear that God's eternal choice does not rest upon individual persons but a group of people. Indeed, it seems perfectly acceptable to say that a part of what God predetermines is that he will have a people until himself. Scripture uses the terms election, chosen people, remnant, etc., to refer to this group. Even in Paul, God's choice always seems to center upon a group of people. However, the New Testament does include within the concept of corporate election, the eternal choice of an individual person. Moreover, the chosen people of God are defined exclusively in terms of God's election of this one person; and that person is Christ.

Electing a Person

One of the differences between election in the Old Testament and the New Testament is that the latter views Christ as the foundation of election. What this suggests is that the person of Christ becomes the focus of God's eternal choice. God predetermines that Christ will be one through whom the world will be reconciled. Consequently, God's chosen people are defined by virtue of their connection to God's chosen messiah. But this is not all. If we understand *who* Christ is, we can detect another side to his election. Christ not only is fully human, he is also fully divine. He is both the human being who is chosen by God and the God who chooses wrapped up in one. To see Christ as the foundation of our election, we must consider both the fact that he defines God's elect people and that he reveals himself as the God who elects and the human who is elected.

The idea that Christ is both the God who chooses and the human being who is chosen comes from a Swiss German theologian named Karl Barth.[9] In his approach to predestination, Barth focuses on how the New Testament centers election upon Christ, especially in light of the fact that Christ is fully God and fully man. When we view Christ as fully God we are focusing on his complete equality with the Father and his absolute divinity. Christ is the eternal Word of God who was with God in the beginning God (John 1:1) and who is the exact representation of the being of God (Heb. 1:3). As the eternal Word of God, Christ participates in God's decision to elect. By viewing Christ as fully human, we are recognizing his complete equality with all humans. Christ is Jesus of Nazareth, the human being who lived, died on a cross and was raised from the dead. Like two sides of the same coin,

9. See Karl Barth, *Church Dogmatics*, vol. 2, part 2, eds. G. W. Bromiley and T. F. Torrance (Edinburgh: T & T Clark, 1957).

Christ's divinity and humanity are the two aspects of his identity and we must always keep this before us. Unless Christ is fully divine, we have no guarantee that God is establishing true fellowship with us; unless Christ is fully human, we have no guarantee that we have true fellowship with God.

In the Incarnation, God builds a bridge of salvation between humanity and divinity. In fact, one could say that the Incarnation *is* the bridge God builds. The Incarnation is nothing less than the eternal Son of God, the second person of the Trinity becoming a human being. The very word "incarnation" means to be in-fleshed or to take on flesh. Barth believes that one can see God's eternal election in the decision of the Son of God to become a human. If the eternal Son is truly God, then God's decision to choose must be made by the Son as well as the Father and the Spirit. It is a decision made by the Triune God who is Father, Son and Holy Spirit. What then is that decision? Is it a secret decision to save some and reject others? Barth's answer is an emphatic No! As he states, "the eternal will of God in the election of Jesus Christ is His will to give Himself for the sake of man as created by Him and fallen from Him. According to the Bible this was what took place in the incarnation of the Son of God, in his death and passion, in His resurrection from the dead. We must think of this as the content of the eternal divine predestination."[10] God's eternal choice is nothing less than to give his own life for others by becoming Jesus of Nazareth. "For God so loved

10. Ibid., 161.

the world that he gave his only begotten Son... (John 3:16). Examining election from the perspective of Christ reveals that divine election is the Son of God's eternal choice to build a bridge by taking on flesh.

If the decision is to become a human being, who is the one chosen? The answer is simple: the particular human being the Son of God became. While the Old Testament sees Israel as the one chosen to be the elect people of God, the New Testament suggests that Christ is the one chosen. In choosing to become a human being, the eternal Son of God was choosing to save the world in and through Jesus. Notice how 1 Peter 1:20 puts it: "He was destined before the foundation of the world, but was revealed at the end of times for your sake." In this statement, Peter places the coming of Christ firmly in God's eternal election.[11] It was a part of God's plan from the very beginning to choose the world through Jesus Christ. In Peter, we find the human side of God's choice. The eternal Son of God chose to become a particular human being, Jesus of Nazareth. In making this eternal choice, God was choosing to save the world through the one Christ, who as fully divine and fully human is the only one suitable to build the bridge.

There is an important practical point to Barth's emphasis on Christ. We can be assured that God's election extends to us

---

11. See I. Howard Marshall, *1 Peter*, The IVP New Testament Commentary Series, ed. G. R. Osborne (Downers Grove, IL: InterVarsity Press, 1991), 55-7; and Andrew Chester and Ralph P. Martin, *The Theology of the Letters of James, Peter, and Jude* (Cambridge: Cambridge University Press, 1994), 108-09.

because of Christ. For Barth, there is no secret will of God predetermining who will go to heaven and who will not go to heaven because God makes his will known in Christ. To put it another way, Christ *is* the God who chooses so if you want to know God's will you need only look at Christ. Secondly, we don't need to worry about *who* gets chosen by God because we know that Christ is the one chosen. Again, there is no secret number of elect God has selected from among the peoples of the earth. God has selected Christ. He is the one individual whose destiny God has determined. In fact, Barth will declare that in and through Christ we can see God's divine Yes to humanity.[12]

When the eternal Son of God *chose* to take on human flesh and become a man, he was saying, "I choose humanity in this one man, Jesus of Nazareth." This is the divine Yes. As Paul puts it, "For the Son of God, Jesus Christ, whom we proclaimed among you... was not 'Yes' and 'No'; but *in him* it is always 'Yes.' For *in him* every one of God's promises is a 'Yes'" (2 Cor. 1:19-20).

God's promises become available to humanity because the election of God moves from Christ to Christ to us (see diagram). By putting together those two ideas the picture we get is that the eternal Son of God, the second person the Trinity has chosen to become a human being so that in the eternal election to be Jesus of Nazareth he might save the whole world. Far from being a dark decision, God's eternal

---

12. Barth, *Church Dogmatics*, vol. 2, part 2, 169ff.

election ought to give us the complete assurance and comfort that God is always working for us not against us.

God's Election to Build a Bridge through the Person of Christ

From Christ as God⇨   To Christ as man⇨   To all those "in Christ"
(The elect Body of Christ)

As the one chosen by God to restore fellowship with humanity, Christ now defines the chosen people of God. When I say that Christ *defines* the chosen people of God, I simply mean that we can *identify* who the elect are in reference to Christ. I can identify myself as a part of God's elect because I belong to Christ and Christ belongs to me. The New Testament describes this connection to Christ primarily in terms of being united to Christ. Throughout Paul's letters one finds numerous references to being "in Christ," "in him," "in whom" and "in Christ Jesus" all of which point toward our union with Christ. We can see the connection between election and Christ most clearly in Ephesians where Paul declares that believers have been chosen *in Christ* before the foundation of the world (1:4). The gospel of John uses the language of "abiding" or "remaining" to describe the union between Christ and believers. This is especially the case in John 15 where Jesus describes himself as the true vine that all believers must abide in like branches. As one commentator suggests, "Jesus redefines the elect as those who abide in him."[13] Even in 1 Peter, we find the idea that God "has called

---

13. See Larry W. Hurtado, *Lord Jesus Christ: Devotion to Jesus in Earliest Christianity* (Grand Rapids, MI: Eerdmans, 2003), 373.

you to his eternal glory *in Christ...* " (5:10). In all of these passages, individuals become a part of God's elect as they become united to Christ and so form a part of his body.

Now that we have examined the role of Christ, I hope that it is becoming clear how God's election of a people and God's election of a person work together. God has chosen in eternity that he will have a people. This much should be clear from our examination of the Old Testament and Romans. However, God has also predestined Christ to be the one who will save the world. All those who become united to Christ share or participate in God's election of Christ. He is the vine and believers are the branches grafted on to his life, death and resurrection. Once grafted on to Christ, we become the corporate body of Christ, the chosen ones from every tribe, nation and tongue. Election is still corporate, but the corporation is defined by Christ and not by national Israel. All of this leads us to the final part of God's eternal election: his plan.

Electing a Plan

God's election of a people and a person naturally tells us that God has always had a plan. The plan speaks to how individuals become a part of God's chosen people. This is the third element in divine election. In choosing Christ to be the one slain from the foundation of the world, God also chooses the means of salvation or the way individuals will bring about their salvation. Given the previous discussion, I need only point out two essential components to this plan. First, God decides that Christ will be the way of salvation ("I am the way, the truth and the life"). Second, God also eternally wills that all those who express faith in Christ will be saved or become a part of God's chosen people. Both of these components represent God's election of a people and a person with one exception, faith as the means to lay hold of Christ. So God not only predestines that Christ be the way, the truth and the life, and that all those who are "in Christ" will be his elect, he also predestines faith as the way to unlock the benefits of Christ's life, death and resurrection (see diagram).

What God Predestines

A People	A Person	A Plan
God will have a chosen people (corporate election)	Christ as God chooses to create a people when he becomes a human being who dies for the whole world	The chosen people of God are all those believe on the Lord Jesus Christ and so are united to him

God invites the entire world to become a part of the body of Christ. He does not single out one group of persons over another as the special recipients of his election. The divine choice from all eternity is that God will have a chosen people who come into existence as they embrace Christ, the chosen one of God by faith. Moreover, as we have seen, the doctrine of election is God's divine Yes to humanity. Rather than working against the pursuit of holiness, we should see election and predestination as giving us the comfort we need to pursue holiness. Why? Because election tells us that God has already built the bridge between humanity and divinity in Christ. Before we existed God was working all things together for our ultimate good by deciding that he himself would seek us out to transform us into his likeness, to heal our disease and to restore fellowship with him. God exercises his providence or care for his creation by joining himself to it in and through Christ and taking its sorrows upon himself. "For he was wounded for our transgressions, he was bruised for our iniquities; the chastisement that brought us peace (*shalom*) was upon him, and by his stripes we are healed" (Is. 53:5). One can see how suffering gives way to a kind of healing that produces wholeness and reconciliation in that the chastisement of God's servant brought peace (*shalom*).[14] Election also tells us that the transformation from one diseased by sin to one healed and holy concerns our becoming the image of Christ who himself is the image of the invisible God (Col. 1:15). Finally, it tells us firmly that our restoration of fellowship is a cooperative affair with God. In and through the God-man, Jesus Christ, God has predetermined to enter into a partnership with humanity in order to bring about our salvation.

---

14. See J. Blenkinsopp, *Isaiah 40-55*, The Anchor Bible (New York, NY: Doubleday, 2000), 352-3.

Chapter 6
Divine Grace and Human Cooperation

For this I toil and struggle with all the energy
that he powerfully inspires within me.

(Col. 1:29, NRSV)

One of the main purposes behind the doctrine of eternal election is to show that salvation remains a work of God's free grace. Election indicates that God was working to bring us to salvation long before we decided to embrace Christ. The fact that God works first and that all our work is merely a response to His prior initiatives tells us that we are saved by grace, not of ourselves "lest anyone should boast" (Eph. 2:8-9, *NKJV*). Nevertheless, we also have a role to play in our salvation even if that role is secondary to the primary role God plays. We must cooperate with God at every step of the process in order to complete our salvation.

God's fundamental call for us to realize our complete potential as those created in the image of God requires that we participate in what God wants to do. God has invited us to share in a divine/human partnership whereby we follow His lead even as He guides and empowers us. The ultimate result of this divine/human partnership is that God helps us to realize His purpose for our lives and so come to flourish as human beings. It is a partnership in which God receives the glory and we receive the good. While eternal election means salvation is always a free work of grace, it does not rule out

God asking us to respond continuously to His gracious initiatives in our lives.

So far, so good. The question is, "how does this work?" How does God work first in our lives and then we respond to what God is doing? This chapter explores the relationship between God's graciously working in the lives of individuals and the need for those same individuals to respond to God. Throughout my discussion, I will maintain that we must cooperate with God at every level and every step of the journey. This is indeed a divine/human partnership. Our cooperation remains contingent upon the Holy Spirit's prior working and occurs primarily as we bring our choices into harmony with God's will for our lives. By gradually aligning our choices with God's choices for us, made known through the Spirit's prompting and guidance, slowly, over the course of our lives, we become more holy and begin to develop the character of God.

One of the misguided ideas I have tried to address is that salvation is equal to forgiveness of sins and gaining admittance into heaven. Instead, salvation is much broader, involving our complete restoration and the full realization of all that we can become in Christ through the power of the Holy Spirit. Certainly, forgiveness is how God initiates restoration and helps us stay on the path of restoration, but that is only one dimension of salvation. If we think of salvation as a complete restoration made possible through our pursuit of holiness, we can begin to understand how it requires a process of transformation in which we become more like God. We become holy and happy. We can also begin to see that our transformation as individual believers goes hand in hand with God's desire to transform the entire cosmos, creating a new heaven and a new earth. Consequently, we need to think about salvation as a journey that we make—a transforming journey in which grace pushes us forward as we choose to work with grace.

The Medicine of Salvation

There is an old illustration going back to the Middle Ages about how God works to bring about salvation in the life of every person. The illustration stems from the idea of receiving a dose of medicine in order to cure a disease. Recall for a moment that in chapter one I discussed sin as a disease and the various ways in which that disease affects us. As I said then, a disease must be cured. In chapter three, I discussed how Christ and the Spirit become the divine medicine God pours forth into our lives to heal us. This medicine has transforming effects when it is applied to our lives. However, we need to consider more carefully the nature of our disease. While some diseases can be cured through a one-time surgery, others require a lengthy process in which an individual must take medication to restore the body to complete health. In a similar way, the salvation wrought for us by Christ and the Spirit requires a lengthy process in which the grace of God slowly but surely restores us to complete health.

When we consider how God works to cure the disease of sin, it might be helpful to consider the way a drug works with the body. Some diseases are just too powerful for the body to fight off by itself. Our immune systems need additional help to combat certain diseases and to restore our physical bodies to complete health. Sometimes doctors will prescribe antibiotics to help our immune system do its job of ridding the body of infections, viruses and other diseases. In addition, we take antibiotics over a period of time and not all at once. I have a young daughter who has battled various infections in her brief life. When the infection becomes too much for her tiny immune system to handle, the doctor will prescribe an antibiotic that we must administer to her over a two-week period. Slowly the antibiotic helps her body fight off the infectious disease. Although she could not overcome the infection on her own, it is important to see that her immune system cooperates or works together with the antibiotic to cure her. In this way, a partnership is created between the antibiotic and the immune system that restores the body to health and returns it to wholeness.

This illustration helps us begin to see how God works with us to cure the disease of sin. First, antibiotics empower our immune system so that it can work to heal the body. In one sense, the immune system continues to work, but it can only succeed with the prior help of the antibiotics. Likewise, God dispenses his grace to us through the work of Christ and in the power of the Spirit thus enabling us to overcome sin. Christ and the Spirit are the divine medicine communicated in order to rid the world of sin. Christ lived a holy life, suffered, died and was raised again to redeem us from the sickness of sin and to restore us to wholeness. The Spirit conforms us to Christ by empowering us to live a holy life, helping us to die daily and, finally, resurrecting us. It is only after the resurrection of our bodies that we become fully healed and fully whole. During this process of healing, we must cooperate with God's grace to overcome sin, i.e., we must cooperate with the Holy Spirit who brings Christ to us and conforms our lives to Christ. However, it is important to keep in mind that all our cooperation remains contingent upon God first dispensing the required medicine.

Secondly, our disease is not immediately cured. Complete healing occurs only after a long period of time in which God repeatedly administers medicine to us and we repeatedly choose to cooperate with that medicine. As I pointed out in chapter three, conversion means more than the initial acceptance of Christ. Instead, it is a lifelong endeavor in which we attempt to become complete disciples of Christ in all that we say and do. This implies that salvation concerns our slow healing as we work in conjunction with the Spirit to become conformed to Christ and so freed of sin's destructive power. Hence we need daily doses of God's grace if we are to be cured completely. We cannot die daily to sin and be made alive unto Christ Jesus without a fresh inpouring of God's Spirit, who guides and enables us to choose righteous lives.

These daily doses of grace from the Holy Spirit serve to bring about our healing over the long haul, or our complete transformation from a child of the devil to a child of God. Keep in mind that God wants to make us *real* sons and daughters and not simply *legal* sons and daughters. This cannot happen without change, being conformed to the image and likeness of God's eternal Son, Jesus Christ. We become conformed to Christ gradually as we receive and act in cooperation with the daily dose of medicine God administers by the power of the Holy Spirit.

Christ and the Spirit as God's Transforming Medicine

Let's step back for a moment and consider more carefully how Christ and the Spirit become the divine medicine God uses to cleanse or sanctify us from the corrupting disease of sin. Our conversion to a new way of living remains directly dependent upon the prior work of Christ and the Spirit. But what about their mutual work brings our healing? Since I have already talked about how Christ and the Spirit lead humanity on a new exodus, I do not want to rehearse that material. Instead, I want to focus more on the cross and resurrection of Christ in relationship to our own transformation from death to life. If we can get a clear sense of the relationship between the prior work of Christ and the Spirit and our transformation, then we will be in a better position to understand the gracious side of salvation.

All Christians agree that on the cross Christ was making atonement for the sins of the world. Many theologians see the cross solely as God's extension of forgiveness because Jesus atoned for our sins. The work of Christ on the cross is just simply about forgiveness and no more. While it is important to see the cross as the place where Jesus endures the penalty for sin, we could look at the cross from a different perspective by asking a different set of questions. Is there a relationship between the penalty for sin and the disease of sin? If so, how does Christ's atonement cure us from the disease of sin? What is it about the death of Christ that supplies our cure? Is there some way in which God's healing medicine gets communicated through the cross?

To answer these questions, we need to look more carefully at certain passages of scripture. A good place to begin is with Paul's claim that God "made him who knew no sin to be sin on our behalf so that in him we might become the righteousness of God" (2 Cor. 5:21). It is clear from the passage that Paul has in view a connection between Christ and the sinner such that Christ became sin that the sinner "in him" might become righteous. What does Paul mean by Christ becoming sin? At minimum, we can say that the place where Christ became sin was on the cross. To say that Christ became sin on the cross also helps us rule out a sinful life. Christ perfectly obeyed the Father and therefore lived a life free from sinful actions. However, this does not answer the question. We still need to determine what it means for Christ to become sin.

Paul's explanation in Romans 6 may provide the clue we need to answer the question. The primary theme in this chapter is how believers are freed from slavery to sin through the death of Christ. For Paul, sin enslaves human beings because it functions as an internal power preventing them from doing what they should. As I mentioned previously, when Paul describes sin as an internal power that reigns through corrupt desires, we should think of a disease. With this in mind, we can better understand Paul when he says, "Now if we died with Christ, we believe that we shall also live with Him, knowing that Christ, having been raised from the dead, dies no more. Death no longer has dominion over Him. For the death that He died, He died to sin once for all; but the life that He lives, He lives to God" (Rom. 6:8-10; *NKJV*). The climax of these verses is v. 10 where Paul says that Christ died to sin once for all and now lives unto God. Christ ends the grip of the disease of sin upon humanity through his own death.[1] In addition, those who participate in Christ's death ("if we died with Christ"), begin to share his life-giving power and so are made free from sin's enslavement. What we could say is that Paul believes Christ experienced the full fury of the disease on the cross because Christ died. The claim that Christ became sin in 2 Cor. 5:21 is no more than Paul's assertion that on the cross Christ became subject to the consequences of sin ("for the wages of sin is death").[2] He is breaking the power of sin by participating in the disease itself to the point that he allows himself to experience its ultimate consequences. As Isaiah 53 suggests, "he was wounded for our transgressions, he was bruised for our iniquities... and he bore the sin of many" (vs. 5, 12). Romans 6 brings out that the death of Christ was about his triumph over the disease of sin by taking it upon himself.

The book of Hebrews puts forward a similar idea about Christ's death. In particular, Hebrews 9 and 10 argue that Christ's sacrificial death is superior to the sacrifices of the Old Testament because it "perfects" believers by "cleansing their

---

1. See J. Ziesler, *Paul's Letter to the Romans*, TPI New Testament Commentaries (Philadelphia, PA: Trinity Press International, 1989), 161-62.
2. J. Murphy-O'Connor, *The Theology of the Second Letter to the Corinthians* (Cambridge: Cambridge University Press, 1991), 61-62.

consciences" once and for all (Heb. 9:14; 10:2, 10, 14). The writer answers the question of what it means to have one's conscience cleansed when he claims that Christ's death removes consciousness of sin (10:2). This suggests that the death of Christ has a healing effect on believers. The healing effect is the removal of our own awareness that we are sinners.[3] The blood of Christ not only becomes the channel of God's forgiveness, but through that forgiveness serves to erase the memory of sin. The purpose of this removal of sin is to give us confidence to worship God through prayer, praise and a lifetime of obedience (see Heb. 10:19-25; 13:15-16). Christ's death heals us initially by removing the barrier that blocks true worship, which is the guilt we experience as a result of our awareness that we have sinned before God.

While removal of our awareness of sin is the primary focus for the writer of Hebrews, it is not the only healing effect of Christ's death that he wants to highlight. He also states, "For by one offering He has perfected forever those who are *being* sanctified" (10:14). The one offering of Christ has perfected those who now seek to approach God by cleansing their conscience of sin. This is the initial healing effect. Christ's sacrifice also has ongoing effects in the lives of believers or those who are "being sanctified." That is, Christ's death continues to sanctify believers over the course of their lives. How does Christ's death continue to sanctify? The writer immediately quotes Jeremiah 31 to suggest that

---

3. See David A. Peterson, *Hebrews and Perfection: An Examination of the Concept of Perfection in the Epistle to the Hebrews* (Cambridge: Cambridge University Press, 1982), 140, 166-67; and Attridge, *Hebrews*, 280-81.

through Christ God is writing his law upon the hearts of believers and remembering their sins no more (Heb. 10:15-17). What one discovers is that there are two healing effects of Christ's death. The first is immediate (cleansing the conscience) and serves to remove any barrier on the part of the believer while the second is ongoing (creating a new heart) and follows from the first. These two effects are bound up with one another in that God begins to create a new heart by removing our own awareness of our sins and then continues that work. Both effects are a resulting of the sanctifying presence of the blood of Christ.

The importance of Christ's blood sacrifice has to do with the life of God. In Leviticus 17:11, God prohibits the Israelites from eating meat with blood still in it because "the life of the flesh is in the blood and I have assigned it to you for making expiation for your lives upon the altar" (*Tanakh*). The same passage goes on to say that "it is the blood, as life, that effects expiation" (*Tanakh*). In the Old Testament, God employed blood sacrifices because blood symbolized the transferal of life. The life of the animal was exchanged for the life of the person. The significance of this for Christ's death is that it suggests to us that in the shedding of Christ's blood the very life of God was being poured out for us. Christ's blood has a sanctifying effect because it is the way God has chosen to communicate his life to us ("The life of the flesh is in the blood"). As his blood covers our sinful conscience, it has healing effects because it is really Christ's life that is cleansing and removing the disease of sin with its accompanying guilt. No wonder that people sing, "The Blood Will Never Lose Its

Power," because the blood of Christ is the channel of God's own powerful life healing us in the midst of our weakness.

What are we to make of all this? Christ's death heals us from the disease of sin by breaking the power of sin, cleansing our conscience and creating in us (over the long haul) a new heart. That is, Christ's death has a transforming effect in our lives. The love of God communicated in and through the cross is about the healing of the nations, and the healing of the disease of sin. To cure the disease of sin fully, Christ must take sin upon himself in order to destroy it. We might think of guilt as a symptom of the disease. If God were simply to treat our guilt, it would like trying to cure pneumonia in the person with AIDS. The deeper problem is AIDS not pneumonia. Pneumonia is simply an effect of AIDS. In the same way, our guilt is the effect of the disease of sin. For God to heal us, he must do more than remove the symptom, he must deal with the underlying disease that manifests itself in the symptom. Of course, in order to deal with the deeper disease doctors must correct the symptoms. Pneumonia itself is a serious problem that must be treated. Any doctor knows that he must take care of the pneumonia so that the patient can be strong enough to endure the treatment for AIDS. While AIDS remains the underlying cause, pneumonia is the immediate threat that must be dealt with. On the cross, Christ certainly was dealing with guilt as a serious symptom of our disease. However, his primary mission was and is to cure the disease since it is the underlying cause of guilt. Without the disease of sin prompting us to engage in sinful and self-destructive behavior, there would be no guilt. The cross is not simply about the removal of guilt nor is it about God identifying with us in our suffering. Instead, it is about God absorbing our sin into his life and destroying it by the power of that life.

Let me make this point by thinking through the AIDS illustration a little more. If I were sick with HIV and it had developed into AIDS, I would not want my father to be injected with the virus just to show me how much he loved me. I would not want my father to suffer and experience the pain of AIDS to prove the intensity of his love, as though unless my father entered into my suffering I could not be convinced of his love. However, if my father somehow had a special property in his immune system that, once injected with HIV, would allow him to build up the appropriate antibodies in order to defeat the disease. And if, upon receiving that injection, my father would be making it possible for me to be cured, then I could understand why he would undertake the ordeal, even if his undertaking of that ordeal meant great pain and suffering on his part as he endured the full onslaught of AIDS. If through his own torment and pain, he was actually defeating the virus and providing a cure so that I could defeat it, so that my suffering could end, then his action would not only display the depth of his love for me, but it would also become the means of my own healing. This is what Christ's death accomplishes for us. It is not simply a magnificent display of divine love, it also represents the power of God to take our disease and the suffering it produces upon himself and destroy it. No wonder Paul could say of God's love: "For I am convinced that neither death, nor life, nor angels, nor rulers, nor things present, nor things to come, nor powers, nor height, nor depth, nor anything else in all creation, will be able to separate us from the love of God in Christ Jesus our Lord" (Romans 8.38-9).

The remedy for our disease is not simply the death of Christ but his life, death *and* resurrection. We know that God's medicine works only because we know that Christ's taking upon himself of our sinful disease does not end with his death but with his triumphant resurrected life. The resurrection of Christ communicates to us that the life of God is indeed pouring forth in and through Christ. God's life is our antidote. It is the cure because God's life powerfully overcomes all things. Moreover, the life of God is poured into our lives through the Holy Spirit who is the Spirit of life. The very same Spirit of God who raised Christ from the dead by pouring out God's own divine power now works in believers empowering them to live and overcome. On the one hand, Christ and the Spirit are the divine medicine. On the other hand, they are the divine medicine because they are fully God. God's life is poured forth to us through the eternal Son of God and the eternal Spirit of God.

Notice how Paul puts it, "And if Christ is in you, the body is dead because of sin, but the Spirit is life because of righteousness. But if the Spirit of Him [God] who raised Jesus from the dead dwells in you, He who raised Christ from the dead will also give life to your mortal bodies through His Spirit who dwells in you" (Rom. 8:10-11). What we find in these two verses is the connection between the work of Christ and the Spirit. If the final end of sin is death, then the ultimate cure must be new life or new creation. In this passage, Paul

145

asserts that God was at work in Christ's death on the cross and in raising Christ from the dead by means of the Holy Spirit in order to cure humanity. The cure is nothing less than God's own life pouring forth into our lives and reviving us.

Paul goes on to declare that we have the "first fruits of the Spirit" (8:23), which means that the Spirit is our guarantee that God's life is at work in us. This same Spirit was at work in Christ raising him from the dead and making him the "first fruits of those who have fallen asleep" (1 Cor. 15:20). If Paul tells us that the Spirit is the "down payment" that the cure is being administered, he also wants us to see that this cure culminates in our own bodily resurrection. In the end, we will be fully healed when "death is swallowed up in victory" because "this corruptible must put on incorruptible and this mortal must put on immortality" (1 Cor. 15:53-54). The end of the process of transformation is resurrection. Until we arrive at that point, the Spirit of life is at work pushing us toward it by helping us in our present life to die to sin. God's cure, then, centers upon the work of Christ and the Spirit because they are the exclusive dispensers of the divine medicine. This medicine cures us of the disease of sin and all of its effects.

When we see how it is that God cures us, we cannot help but be led to the conclusion that salvation is a work of grace. How can we be cured if we do not have the proper medicine? Our spiritual immune systems are simply unable to overcome the powerful effects of sin. The conclusion must be that we cannot cure ourselves. Yet, we can and do participate in God's cure. Since salvation is about our complete transformation from one diseased by sin to one healed by grace, then we

146

should see how our cooperation is essential to that transformation. God's medicine must be applied to our lives. It must be dispensed to us and we must accept it.

How God Dispenses the Medicine

In one sense, I've already answered the question of how God dispenses the medicine of salvation. The work of Christ and the Spirit is the spiritual antibiotic God has for us. However, this antibiotic still must be *applied* to our lives. The difference is between developing an antibiotic and then administering that antibiotic to individuals. The work of Christ and the Spirit I just described deals with how God develops the cure, but God must also apply it. This is the question we must now address. How does God dispense the divine medicine to us in such a way that salvation is always a work of grace and yet we must cooperate with this work? To answer this question, it is not enough simply to assert that we must make a choice. We need to consider how it is that we can choose even while we are diseased.

The simple answer is that the Spirit enables us to choose. John's Gospel tells us that to be born again is to be born of the Spirit (John 3:5-8). It is the Spirit who gives birth to the new life Christians begin to experience in Christ. The Spirit initiates new birth through convicting the world of sin (John 16:8-9). That is, the Spirit awakens people to the reality that they are indeed diseased. To put it in Paul's terms, the Spirit must remove the veil by which the god of this world has blinded the hearts of men and women (2 Cor. 3:12-4:6). The blindness produced by sinful patterns of behavior prevents

147

people from recognizing even the need to be cured. In the same way that an alcoholic must first be convinced that he has a problem, sinners must first be convinced that they are diseased. However, the Spirit must not only convince us that we are diseased, he must also empower us to choose. It is one thing to recognize the truth, it is quite another to act on it. The Spirit must help us do both.

Before moving any further in our discussion, let me make a simple but important point. God leaves no one out when dispensing his medicine. Everyone gets a dose. By declaring, "For God so loved the world that he gave his only begotten Son that whosoever should believe in him will not perish but have everlasting life" (3:16), John's Gospel is telling us that God extends salvation to everyone. "Whosoever" means "whosoever," which implies that God gives his medicine to the entire world. The call to salvation is a universal call that goes out to every person.

I can hear the initial protest that if God dispenses his medicine to everyone then everyone must be saved. Not at all. It should be clear by now that salvation is about our complete healing, which means that one dose of medicine will not due. So, when I say that God dispenses his medicine to everyone, I simply mean that God gives the initial dose freely to all. John Wesley refers to the initial dose as prevenient grace because he thought God supplies some grace beforehand to enable us to choose him.[4] However, that does not mean that everyone

4. See Wesley's sermon, "On Working Out Your Own Salvation" in *John Wesley's Sermons: An Anthology*, ed. A. C. Outler and R. P. Heitzenrater (Nashville, TN: Abingdon Press, 1991), 485-92. For an explanation of Wesley's

chooses to cooperate with God. Some receive the initial dose and then decide that they don't need any more. If salvation depends upon our cooperation, then we can choose not to cooperate. We can refuse God's treatment.

Let me return to the medicine illustration to make the point clearer. Imagine that God walked into a hospital filled with terminally ill patients. The patients are terminally ill because, unless they receive some miraculous cure, their disease will eventually take their lives. As if this were not bad enough, let's also say that these patients are in a coma. Their disease is so bad that they have lost consciousness. What is God's response? Does God wait for them to respond to him knowing that they cannot regain consciousness on their own? Or, does God give them an initial dose of medicine? I would suggest that God does the latter. There is no waiting for people to do something they cannot do. Instead, God invites the entire world receive his cure by taking the initiative and administering the first dose of medicine.

What does that first dose accomplish? It restores consciousness to the patients such that they can see and understand their condition. They can also understand that they require *additional* doses of medicine to complete their treatment. As I mentioned earlier, some diseases are simply too powerful to overcome with a single dose of medicine. They require long-term treatment. Since salvation is about complete transformation, we know that it too requires long-

doctrine of prevenient grace, see Kenneth J. Collins, *The Scripture Way of Salvation: The Heart of John Wesley's Theology* (Nashville, TN: Abingdon Press, 1997), 38-45.

term treatment. The initial dose is to get the patient to the point where a choice is possible. Is the patient compelled to continue treatment? No. The cure is offered but the patient must decide to receive the medicine. In addition, the patient must decide over and over again to receive God's medicine. She must die daily to sin and be made alive unto righteous, which means that she must ask God to give her additional doses every day. The first dose helps people make the choice, but that's all.

Thus far I've given an illustration to talk about how God dispenses the first dose of medicine to everyone. The question I must now address is where this actually happens. Can we point to real life scenarios where God is actually dispensing his medicine? For the sake of space, I will only offer one example although I think there are a lot of ways that God can and does dispense his medicine. However, let me offer a description of what happens on Sunday mornings as pastors deliver their sermons because I think that is a clear place where everyone would agree God is dispensing his medicine. Pastors are clear examples of ambassadors of Christ through whom God makes his appeal to the world or through whom God dispenses his medicine (see 2 Cor. 5:20). If understood correctly, we could say that the delivery of a sermon is also the dispensing of divine medicine.

When pastors deliver their sermons on Sunday morning, they are attempting to communicate the message of the gospel to their audiences. The question is how can any pastor really communicate the gospel in such a way that it connects to every individual in the audience? The answer is that no pastor can. Even in a church of fifty people, it is almost impossible to preach a sermon that will connect with every one of them. Why? Because every person is dealing with different issues. It is not humanly possible to preach a sermon that will speak to every issue.

In addition, most pastors recognize that even their best sermons may not reach anyone. Sometimes people just don't respond.

To understand how it is that any one responds to a sermon, we need to consider the work of the Spirit. When a message goes forth from the pulpit, it takes on a life of its own because the Spirit begins to work in and through the message. While it is impossible for a human being to communicate a message that will speak to fifty others, it is certainly possible for the Spirit. The Spirit knows the inner thoughts of each heart and is fully capable of applying the sermon to every heart even if the pastor is not. Even one phrase from the lips of a pastor can penetrate the heart of a particular person if the Spirit is at work. I have witnessed numerous times where a pastor has uttered one phrase like, "God is sovereign," and that one phrase has impacted an individual more than anything else the pastor said. Theologians have described this as the difference between the external call of God and the internal call of God. The external call has to do with the sermon that goes forth from the pulpit and exists outside of the hearers. The internal call refers to the word that the Spirit speaks inside the mind of the hearers. The Spirit empowers the listener to choose by applying the message to her life in a way that resonates with the issues she is facing. She responds because in her heart, "God is sovereign," causes her to consider the ways in which she has not surrendered her life. This is the work of the Holy Spirit dispensing God's own medicine.

Have you ever had a moment of insight into your own life? A time where you came to see the truth about who you are and what you need. For the first time, you saw things clearly. What generates this moment of insight? I would suggest that these moments of insight into our lives are Spirit-inspired. They are the ways that the Spirit works in our hearts to open our eyes so that we can see the truth. This can and does happen through sermons, but it can also happen in other ways. It can even happen by a friend just giving us a piece of advice. God uses anything he can to awaken us to the truth about our condition. When we have these moments of insight, we now have a choice. We can choose to act on them or not. We can choose to receive the dose of medicine that God is giving or refuse the treatment. When we choose to live in light of the truth that God communicates to us, we are saying, "God, I accept your medicine and I want more."

How We Respond to the Medicine

Although God is always actively at work in our lives attempting to bring us to Christ, the journey of salvation begins the moment we cooperate with the work of the Holy Spirit. We must choose to respond to the work of God. Following scripture, we can refer to this moment of cooperation as the act of faith. When individuals "believe on the Lord Jesus Christ," that is, when they exercise faith in

152

Christ, they are cooperating with the work of the Spirit. In fact, it is by faith alone that we embrace Christ and by faith alone that we remain connected to Christ.

What does it mean to exercise faith? What are we doing when we believe in Christ for our salvation? Early Protestant theologians described the act of faith in terms of trust in God or heartfelt reliance upon God. To rely on anyone is to place yourself and your well being into the hands of another and this is always a risky venture. The risk involves trusting someone else to do something for us. Sometimes the risk is minimal. I rely on the postal worker to deliver my mail, but if he fails to do so the cost to me is more inconvenience than anything else. At other times, the risk can be great. When a person who has a life-threatening disease visits a doctor, she places herself into his hands, relying upon his medical knowledge and expertise to cure her. To trust God for salvation is the greatest risk of all. It means placing one's personal destiny and spiritual well being into God's hands. Believing in Christ for salvation first involves a reliance or trust upon Christ to do what we cannot do: heal ourselves of the self-destructive choices resulting from the disease of sin.

When Paul says believe on the Lord Jesus Christ and you will be saved, he wants us to trust or rely upon Christ to save us. This leads us to the second part of the act of faith. It is a *heartfelt* reliance upon Christ. The term heartfelt suggests that the commitment to rely upon Christ must be total. The famous Protestant Reformer, Martin Luther describes

153

heartfelt reliance by appealing to the idea of getting on a ship.[5] Luther wants us to think about what it means to step foot on a ship and *trust* that ship to carry us across an ocean so that we arrive safely on the other side.. The moment we put both feet on the ship is the moment we begin to trust. In addition, that trust is total. We are placing our lives into the hands of a large piece of machinery and the crew that runs it. Will the ship do what it claims it will do? Will it get us to the other side of the ocean? This is what it means to have heartfelt reliance. It is when we are invested in God's work. When the ship leaves the dock we know that its journey and our journey must be made together.

It would be a mistake to think of the act of faith as a one-time decision. We must trust that God is indeed at work in our lives, curing us of the disease of sin even when this does not seem to be the case. Both the initial choice to believe and the ongoing response of belief should characterize our lives as Christians if we are to complete this transforming journey. We must trust God because although salvation is a gradual process, it is not always one of forward movement. It's more like one step forward, two steps backward, two steps forward, one step backward. Only when we view the process from the end can we see that we were progressively inching our way to perfection. As long as we remain in the middle of the journey, at times, it can become difficult to tell what God is doing because the journey itself is filled with starts and stops, failures and successes. From beginning to end we must

5. See A. E. McGrath, *Reformation Thought: An Introduction*, third edition (Oxford: Blackwell Publishers, 1999), 111-12.

see what God is doing with the eyes of faith. Hebrews makes it clear that faith is "the assurance of things hoped for, the conviction of things not seen" (11:1; *NRSV*). It is only at the end, when the process is over that faith will give way to full sight and we will no longer see through a mirror darkly but will see God face to face.

Until we see God face to face, we must work, struggling with all of his energy which so powerfully energizes us (Col. 1:29). The cooperation between human freedom and divine grace is at the heart of salvation. Salvation remains a work of grace because by means of Christ and the Spirit God both develops and dispenses the divine medicine. This medicine is the very power of God's indestructible life being given to us. We can only respond to what God has already done and is doing. However, respond we must if we are to be saved completely. We cannot realize our complete potential as human beings apart from God, but neither can we realize it apart from the exercise of our choice. Each time we respond to God's medicine we are trusting him to do what he has promised. One day we will put on immortality and incorruption. One day we will see God. Until then, as Paul tells us, we must struggle on because God struggles on in us and through us.

Chapter 7
Setting the Heart on Fire

As the deer pants for the water brooks,
So pants my soul for You, O God.
My soul thirsts for God, for the living God.

(Psalm 42:1-2a; NKJV)

When we consider that salvation necessitates our complete transformation from one diseased by sin to one healed by grace, we are immediately struck with a potential problem. Anyone who has embarked on a long journey knows that completing the journey requires a great deal of effort and determination. All along the way there are numerous obstacles to overcome. Some obstacles come from inside of us such as when we work against ourselves by making wrong choices. Other obstacles come from outside of us. For example, when we lose someone we love, encounter discrimination because of race or gender, experience conflict in our relationships with others or face life changes like having children, getting laid off of work, etc. These obstacles conspire against us, tiring us and making the journey much more difficult to complete. Many times we think about quitting. We wonder if the journey is worth all the pain and anguish we sometimes experience. In the midst of these obstacles, we must possess the determination and stamina to make it. As Paul reminds us, many runners compete in a race but only one gets the prize (1 Cor. 9:24). Like Paul, we too must run in such a way as to get the prize.

But how? How do we press on? How do we maintain that determination of will which says, "victory shall be mine!"? Even with God's help, pursuing holiness is hard and anyone who thinks differently is either foolish or has never tried to live a holy life. When Paul declares that he presses on toward the goal to win the prize (Phil. 3:14), it seems clear that the journey he is describing is long and demanding. Paul's message of salvation by grace does not exempt him from the difficult work of daily dying to self and becoming alive to Christ in holiness. To overcome the obstacles that impede us, I would suggest that we must allow God continuously to set our hearts on fire with renewed energy and passion. The kind of fire I have in mind is a fire of passion that propels us onward and upward in our quest to see God and so finish the race. It's the passion expressed in Paul's declaration that "whatever gains I had, these I have come to regard as loss because of Christ" (Phil. 3:7). It's the passion of the psalmist who cries out, "For a day in your courts is better than a thousand elsewhere. I would rather be a doorkeeper in the house of my God than live in the tents of wickedness" (Psalm 84:10). It's the passion of a bride who longs for her bridegroom. This passion not only inflames the heart, but melts it and makes it one with Christ. In short, it helps us to fulfill the commandment to love the Lord your God with all of your heart, soul, mind and strength. In this chapter I want to examine how holy passion supplies the fuel that helps us pursue holiness even in the midst of the long and difficult journey of salvation. I also want us to see how we can cultivate our passion for God.

158

Holy Passion as the Fuel of a Holy Life

When we put the idea of salvation as a transforming journey together with a passionate longing for God, it points us toward the marriage between Christ and the believer or the bride and her heavenly bridegroom (cf. Eph. 5:21-33; Rev. 19:7; 21:2, 9; 22:17). Marriage is a lifelong journey of two people who seek to intertwine their hearts and make them one. This goal is not accomplished easily, nor does it happen in a short period of time. Both partners must work hard at learning to love one another and both partners grow and change in the process. In a certain sense, both partners must die to their old ways of living as single persons and embrace new ways of living together as a couple. What helps fuel the hard work of marriage is the fire of passion that each partner has for the other. The passion that both feel for one another helps to consummate their love and solidify it in a long-term commitment, which scripture describes in terms of a covenant.

When I suggest that the fire of passion between spouses helps them solidify their love, I am not implying that this passion is, or even should be, present all the time. Passions are temporary periods of intense emotional activity where our emotions explode outward in attraction or longing toward someone or something else. Sometimes passions erupt spontaneously and unexpectedly, at other times they bubble up from intentional actions on the part of the married couple. Regardless, all couples need to rekindle their passion for one another from time to time in order to further develop a long-term loving disposition. Moreover, rekindling one's passion

159

does not necessarily mean sexual passion, although this is certainly one kind of passion accompanying attraction to another person. What I primarily mean is reminding themselves of those qualities or traits that attracted them to one another and noticing new qualities that emerge in the course of each person's growth and development. Sometimes this can happen in quite simple ways. For example, when I see my wife standing her ground in a debate over a woman's role in the home or in ministry, I am reminded of how attractive I find her courage and strength of mind. Her refusal to be consigned to a certain picture of women is one of the reasons why I am so passionately committed to her. Seeing her courage in action sparks my passion for her and prompts me to draw closer to her. At other times, couples must be intentional about rekindling their passion such as setting aside special times to spend together. In these ways, passion fuels a marriage and enables both partners to press through the difficult times and the hard work of becoming one in heart and mind.

I would suggest that our relationship with Christ works in a similar way. As scripture indicates, we are being united to Christ in marriage by the Spirit. While the final consummation of this marriage awaits Christ's second coming, nevertheless, as Paul makes clear in Ephesians 5, it is also a present reality for believers. Believers together are being united to Christ in preparation for that final consummation. To make this marriage between Christ and the believer last over the long haul, it must be fueled with passion. However, there are important differences between conventional marriages and the marriage between Christ and the believer. In human marriages both partners must learn to love one another, which requires that both change and adapt. In the marriage between Christ and the believer, Christ always remains fully committed to the believer. The believer is the one who must change or adapt as he learns to love and cleave to Christ over the long haul.

Johann von Staupitz, one of Martin Luther's teachers, helps us to see that what keeps us committed to Christ is the love of the Spirit inflaming our hearts and moving us closer and closer toward God. Staupitz suggests that this love does not make *us* pleasing to God, but *God* pleasing to us. He states that believers are,

> ... made alive through faith active in love: that is to say, active through the fire of our love, set afire by the love of Him who is the only perpetual fire, coming down from heaven. All other fires have lost their spell. This fire makes God pleasing and acceptable to us, so that not only what is contrary to God but also that which is not God becomes displeasing to us... Through this love we are and live upright and just, not for ourselves but for God.[1]

---

1. Johann von Staupitz, *Eternal Predestination and its Execution in Time* as found in Heiko Oberman, *Forerunners of the Reformation: The Shape of Late Medieval Thought Illustrated by Key Documents* (Philadelphia, PA: Fortress Press, 1981), 182-3.

We may here think about the fire of holiness that urges us forward in our quest to know God more intimately and so cleave to him. Staupitz captures that Pentecostal passion for holiness by referencing its origin in the love of God shed abroad in the heart of the believer by the power and presence of the Holy Spirit. It is important to observe where Staupitz locates the problem. It is not with God's attitude to the believer, which remains loving; rather the obstacle resides within the believer. The believer must learn to see God as her ultimate good; she must learn to see God as pleasing and acceptable, someone to pursue with the whole heart; in short, she must learn to love God with all of her heart, soul, mind and strength.

Cultivating a Passion for God
The Way Corporate Worship Cultivates Passion

The Pentecostal power to overcome sin, death, disease and the devil resides in the fiery passion of a heart set ablaze by the Holy Spirit. It is the power to press on, to say, "if I hold my peace, let the Lord fight my battles, if I sing and shout, have faith and never doubt, it shall be mine, victory shall be mine." My use of a song to illustrate this point is intentional because worship is one of the primary ways our hearts are set ablaze. Thanksgiving, prayer and praise all contribute to the creation of holy passion. As we worship God, particularly in a worship service, the Spirit helps us bend all of our longings and desires toward heaven. How does that happen? When we enter into the songs of worship, they ignite our passion for

God by reminding us of who God is or what he has done for us. Worship songs and hymns paint a picture of God that bring into focus God's own characteristics helping us to see that God is indeed our ultimate good. The holy passion evoked by these songs or hymns helps us develop a constant affection for God, thus it serves as the fuel of the holy life removing any spiritual paralysis that may beset us and pushing us toward perfection.

Let me further illustrate how worship helps us rekindle holy passion by telling a story. I recall something happening to me one Sunday morning when my church was singing the worship chorus "I See the Lord": "I see the Lord, seated on his throne exalted; and the train of his robe fills the temple with glory; and the whole earth is filled; and the whole earth is filled; and the whole earth is filled with his glory." The song summarizes Isaiah's vision of God in Isaiah 6. As I sang the words that particular morning, I found myself focusing on the Isaiah passage and rehearsing over and over the nature of this majestic God seated upon his throne. I pondered the description of God's robe filling the temple, which conveys the sovereignty and stateliness of the ruler of all creation. For a moment, caught up in that Isaianic vision, I beheld an image of the majesty and glory of the Lord who sovereignly reigns over the earth with perfect power and perfect justice. I saw this one who cannot sin, who always acts uprightly, who delivers his people from their sins, who hears the widow's cries and who is working all things together for the good of his creation. However, my thoughts did not end there.

As I reflected further on the words of the song ("and the whole earth is filled with his glory"), I decided to turn them into a prayer:

Lord, let the whole earth be filled with your glory. Lord, let this kingdom that you have established with your power and might fill the earth, consuming injustice, bringing peace, causing the lion to lie down with the lamb, and restoring everything to its rightful place for YOUR glory. Lord, let this kingdom be established in me; may I reflect your glory and majesty in my life for you are majestic and wondrous to behold.

All of this occurred in a few moments, but it inflamed my heart. I left that service in love with my God all over again and determined to pursue him and the establishment of his kingdom at all costs. This, I believe, is how prayer and praise can come together to form worship, and it is one way our hearts become inflamed for God, the object of our love. Moreover, the primary person behind this is none other than the Holy Spirit. As we worship, the Spirit pours himself out into our hearts and catches us away into a vision of God. We leave worship with a renewed passion for God and his kingdom, our hearts having been wedded to his heart once again, and determined to pursue holiness in our life, in our church and in our world.

As we enter into public worship, we learn to love God by having our passions for God ignited once again. As I have suggested, one can see how hymns and worship choruses help us to renew this passion by reminding us of God's character or actions on our behalf, or by expressing for us the kind of desires we should possess. The contemporary worship chorus "Jesus, Lover of My Soul" provides a good example. The chorus goes like this, "Jesus, lover of my soul, Jesus, I will never let you go. You've taken me from the miry clay, set my feet upon the rock and now I know. I love you, I need you. Though my world may fall, I'll never let you go. My Savior, my closest friend, I will worship you until the very end."[2] The song attempts to arouse our passion for God by reminding us of what Christ has done for us. In this sense, it functions in a way similar to how husbands and wives stir their passion for one another. In the same way that I am moved with passion for my wife when I see her standing her ground in debate, my heart is moved toward God when I remember all that God has done for me in Christ. Another example is the hymn "Great is Thy Faithfulness."

Great is Thy Faithfulness, O God my Father!
There is no shadow of turning with Thee;
Thou changest not, Thy compassions they fail not:
As Thou has been Thou forever will be

Summer and winter and springtime and harvest,
Sun, moon and stars in their courses above,
Join with all nature in manifold witness
To Thy great faithfulness, mercy and love

---

2. *WOW Worship Songbook: Today's 30 Most Powerful Worship Songs* (Mobile, AL: Integrity Incorporated, 2000), 111-15.

Pardon for sin and a peace that endureth,
Thine own dear presence to cheer and to guide,
Strength for today and bright hope for tomorrow,
Blessings all mine, with ten thousand beside

Great is Thy faithfulness! Great is Thy faithfulness!
Morning by morning new mercies I see;
All I have needed Thy hand hath provided,
Great is Thy faithfulness, Lord unto me!

The three stanzas of the hymn all reinforce the primary theme of God's covenant faithfulness or steadfast love. By the time the person sings the chorus for the final time, she has reminded herself of God's unchanging character; how God's care and concern for nature, as evidenced in the constancy of the seasons and the rising and setting of the sun, witnesses to this unchanging character; and finally how this unchanging character ungirds her day by day until she stands with ten thousand in heaven. The hymn offers a picture of God as faithful Father who actively works on his children's behalf. When a believer enters into the words of the hymn, she sees God and yearns to embrace this loving and steadfast Father once again.

While public worship can rekindle our passions for God, there is no automatic guarantee that it will rekindle them every time. We must approach worship in the same way that we approach every other aspect of our relationship to Christ: faith, hope and love. As we lift our voices in song, we must *believe* that the Holy Spirit will make Christ present to us in and through the words. When we sing the words we must *hope* in eager expectation for the coming of our king. Finally, we must draw on the deep reservoir of God's *love* for us, asking the Spirit, who pours this love into our hearts, to raise us above ourselves even as Christ descends to us. By exercising faith, hope and love, we prepare ourselves to receive Christ even on those days when our passions are not ignited.

Intimacy as the Heart of Worship

We all need to be refueled constantly, and I have suggested that this occurs in the context of corporate worship. Let me now broaden the idea of worship beyond a public worship service and define it as *a prayerful posture that finds in God the ultimate fulfillment of all that we are*. When we think of someone having good posture, we are taking note of how the vertebrae in that person's back all align themselves in a correct position. In the same way, good spiritual posture is when our desires align themselves toward God; it is when our desires become fixed upon God. In Sonnet 116, Shakespeare captures defines true love as fixing one's desires upon another person such that they cannot be shaken. He states,

Love is not love,
Which alters when it alteration finds,
Or bends with the remover to remove:
O no!, it is an ever-fixed mark,
That looks on tempests and is never shaken

Love does not alter or change even when the person who is loved changes; nor does love bend and cease when it is not returned. For Shakespeare the power of true love lies in its being "an ever-fixed mark" that does not waver through the changes of life. True love then implies a covenant where one person fixes his desires upon another and refuses to be moved. It is nothing short of a posture or a stand that an individual takes when he declares, "I will love you and no other." This is what it means to fix one's desires.

Fixing one's desires upon God involves the development of a way of thinking about God, that one's life finds its ultimate fulfillment in God. When I say that worship involves a prayerful *posture* I mean that it involves a constant mind set or attitude we have that causes us to cleave to our heavenly bridegroom. "I will love you Lord and no other god." Central to the development of this mind set is a drive to cultivate intimacy with God, which is fueled by setting our hearts on fire with holy passion. When one person desires to be with another, he desires to move into an intimate relationship with that person. With this in mind, let's look at two ways scripture describes the intimate relationship between God and the believer to gain further insight into the nature of worship as a prayerful posture. We find these two ways expressed in Revelation and Galatians. As we examine them briefly, let's keep in mind that these texts help us to develop a prayerful posture by showing us how to cultivate intimacy with God or to fix our desires upon God.

The first text may be found at the end of Revelation where John writes: "And the Spirit and the bride say, 'Come!' And let him who hears say, 'Come!' And let him who thirsts come. Whoever desires, let him take the water of life freely" (22:17). In his work on Revelation, Richard Bauckham identifies two important aspects to this passage.[3] First, the bride identified here is the New Jerusalem, which means the church as she will be at the end of time and not the church in her present state (cf. Rev. 21:2). Second, John invites his readers, including the seven churches of Asia, to be a part of this bride if they will join in the prayer for the bridegroom to come. As John reminds each of the seven churches, "Listen to what the Spirit is saying." The Spirit is saying "Come!" Each church, and therefore each believer, is invited to join her voice to the Spirit's. Consequently, we are engaged in worship when, as the bride of Christ, we can say to our bridegroom with all of our heart, "Come!" The prayer for the bridegroom to come expresses the ardent desire of a bride to unite to her beloved, her first love. It is the language of love that stands behind the request and, as John makes clear, this language is inspired by the Spirit. To yearn for the coming of the bridegroom is to recognize that one's life will find its completion in the divine embrace with Christ. This is how we begin to fix our desires upon God. We ground our longing for Christ's return in our desire to be with Christ, to be in his presence.

To make the same point in a slightly different way, I could just as easily said that we are engaged in worship when we can say to God with all of our heart, "Abba! Father!" The Abba cry shows us another way to fix our desires upon God by

---

3. Richard Bauckham, *The Climax of Prophecy: Studies on the Book of Revelation* (Edinburgh: T & T Clark, 1993), 166-68.

expressing the intimate bond between a child and her father. It testifies to our being children of the Father of Jesus Christ. As Paul indicates, "God has sent the Spirit *of his Son* into our hearts crying, 'Abba! Father!'" (Gal. 4:6). Paul makes a similar point in Romans 8:14-16 where he states, "For as many as are led by the Spirit of God, these are the sons of God. For you did not received the spirit of bondage again to fear, but you received the Spirit of adoption by whom we cry out, 'Abba, Father.' The Spirit Himself bears witness with our spirit that we are the children of God." Gordon Fee suggests that Paul's choice of "Spirit of his Son" in Galatians is no mistake. It indicates to the believer that the Spirit causes her to share in the intimate relationship between Jesus and the Father.[4] Jesus himself addressed God as Abba, and the fact that we, inspired by the Spirit, can utter those words is a sign to us of the intimate relationship God has established with us and the need for us to mature in that relationship. God wants us to know that we are his children and he has poured forth his Spirit as a sign to us of our adoption into his family. Those who respond to the Spirit's prompting with the cry "Abba! Father!" see their Father as having all that they need.

My daughter has a peculiar behavior she expresses to my wife and me when she wants to get close to us. Like all children, sometimes she experiences separation anxiety where she is unsure of our commitment and needs to be

---

4. G. Fee, *God's Empowering Presence*, 404ff. See also J. D. G. Dunn, "Spirit Speech: Reflections on Romans 8:12-27" in *Romans and the People of God: Essays in Honor of Gordon D. Fee on the Occasion of His 65th Birthday*, ed. Sven K. Soderlund and N. T. Wright (Grand Rapids, MI: Eerdmans, 1999), 84.

reassured that we are there for her. Sometimes she just wants to express her affection for us and her need to have us close. During these moments, she will bury her face in my wife's face or my face. She does this by placing her forehead against mine and slowly rocking her head from side to side in a motion like a skater performing a figure eight. In this brief display of affection, there is no need for an exchange of words. The actions clearly communicate my daughter's desire to be intimate with us her parents.

While I am certain that as she grows and matures how she displays affection will change, nevertheless, it is my hope that she will always desire to do so. I think the Abba cry embodies both God's desire for us to display affection for him and our own wish to express affection for our heavenly Father. The way we display that affection is not as important as the fact that we show it. No doubt, our displays of affection will change as we change and the cry "Abba!" will be expressed differently. There may be times in our lives where we need to bury our faces in God's, slowly rocking our head as his Spirit envelops us in the loving embrace of the Father. At other times, we may indicate how much we love God by performing righteous deeds in his name such as evangelizing, taking care of the sick or helping the oppressed. However we express such affection, it is the affection itself that lies beneath the Abba cry and encompasses the heart of worship.

Both "Abba! Father!" and "Come!" can easily be trivialized, but when uttered from the lips of one who desires God they take on a different meaning. Moreover, the difference has everything to do with the *posture* of the person who utters

171

them. Someone who is in love with another human being and is passionately devoted to that person would not see the request to come as trivial. Instead, the request symbolizes that person's deep commitment and desire to be with his beloved. There have been times when my wife and I were separated for long periods. During those times, she has said, "I wish you would *come* home," or, I have said, "I wish I could *come* home." When separated we desire to be with one another and that desire gets expressed in the wish that the other person would come. The wish to come both expresses our desire to be with one another and helps us to continue to fix our desires upon one another. It is one of the ways that we develop a posture of love toward each other.

The same point can be made of "Abba! Father!" The phrase captures a person's desire to express fully the deep commitment of a child for a father. When Paul indicates that we cry out "Abba! Father!" by the Holy Spirit, he seems to be suggesting that the depth of commitment issuing forth in the cry of Abba cannot occur apart from the Spirit's work in one's life. In crying out to God "Abba! Father!" we are learning to fix our desires upon him as the one who has all of the answers to life's questions. No one can express this deep commitment to God in words apart from the Spirit actively igniting their love. The Spirit inflames our hearts to invite the Lord Jesus to come and to cry out "Abba! Father!"

Now, let's bring our brief examination of these passages full circle and look at how they reinforce my definition of worship. Remember, worship is *a prayerful posture that finds in God the ultimate fulfillment of all that we are.* If we consider both passages in the context of our relationship with God, they indicate how we present ourselves as living sacrifices (Rom. 12:1-2). Living sacrifices describe those who dedicate their lives wholly to God because they find the completion of their life in God ("in him we do live and move and have our being") and thus long to be with God. So, worship is a posture that we develop whereby we fix our desires upon God by longing for Christ to come and crying out Abba! Father!

How Prayer Cultivates Intimacy

Yet worship is also a *prayerful* posture. By describing worship as a prayerful posture, I want to convey how prayer contributes to the cultivation of worship by helping us develop "good posture" toward God. While prayer can take on a petitionary tone, it is not simply petitionary or even primarily petitionary. The business of prayer is not asking God for an answer to every want we have. Instead, the primary purpose of prayer resides in the cultivation of intimacy with God. With Christ in the school of prayer means spending time with Christ learning more about him and growing closer and closer to him. Conforming our lives to Christ requires that we cultivate the intimacy necessary to know Christ, and this intimacy begins primarily with prayer. This is how the act of praying develops a prayerful posture that leads to worship. It is in the context of prayer or our conversation with God that we say "come" and cry out "Abba! Father!" In this sense, I like the subtitle of a recent book on prayer, *Finding the Heart's True Home*.[5] As we cultivate intimacy with God in our prayers, we develop a posture of prayer that points us heavenward and keeps us focused on Christ even in the midst of the daily affairs of life.

However, as a good friend reminds me constantly, what does this mean practically? How do we draw closer to Christ in and through prayer? How do we cultivate the intimacy necessary to develop a prayerful posture? Christians constantly talk about spending time in God's presence, but what do they mean? How can we have a conversation with God that is a true dialogue? Let me offer at least two ways in which I think this dialogue can occur.

First, *we dialogue with God by praying through our theology*. All I mean by praying our theology is praying what we believe about God, Christ, the Holy Spirit and a host of other doctrines such as those found in the Church of God Declaration of Faith or other statements of doctrine. Whether we recognize it or not, all Christians have a theology because all Christians believe certain things about God, Jesus, the Spirit, salvation, etc. Of course, our theology should be grounded upon the scriptures, but it is not reducible to the scriptures themselves. One of the first lectures I give my students is on the difference between biblical studies and theology. Biblical studies attempts to understand the concerns of the biblical authors in the context of their own time, whereas theology emerges the moment we bring our own questions to bear on the scriptures.

---

5. Richard Foster, *Prayer: Finding the Heart's True Home* ((New York, NY: HarperOne, 2003).

When James Dobson writes a book on how to deal with a strong-willed child, he is asking a twenty-first century question not a first-century question. To answer this question requires that he engage in theology (with a little child psychology thrown in) not biblical studies. He claims that his advice on raising children is biblical, but what he means is that it accurately reflects what scripture says. Theology becomes biblical when it faithfully reflects what is in scripture. Conversely, theology is unbiblical when it does not faithfully reflect what is in scripture. Jehovah's Witnesses may have a theology but that theology is not a faithful reflection of what the scriptures teach about God, Christ and salvation. Therefore, our theology represents our understanding of who God is and what God is doing in light of the scriptures.

When we pray our theology, we enter into a conversation with God. Our theology helps us to construct a picture of God so that we can know something about who we are addressing in our prayers. To put it differently, what we believe about God and salvation (what God is doing for us) forms a portrait of God that helps us know something of the one to whom we pray. We do not pray to some faceless, shapeless deity, we pray to the God revealed in Jesus Christ. In a similar way, I am married to a real person who has her own unique personality. The only way I can cultivate intimacy with my wife is by taking the time to get to know her. To do so, I must, in a certain sense, *study* her, that is, get to know her personality, her likes and dislikes, her strengths and weaknesses, etc. The more I study my wife, the more intimate our conversations become because those conversations are based on a correct knowledge of her (who she really is). Likewise, we cultivate intimacy with God by taking the time to get to know God. If we want to know something about the one to whom we are praying, we should study theology. The simplest definition of theology is the study of God. In the same way that I get to know my wife by studying what she does and listening to what's important to her, I get to know God by studying God and finding out what's important to God. As Karl Barth reminds us, "Prayer without study would be empty. Study without prayer would be blind."[6] My theology, my study of God helps me to talk to God in prayer and listen to God speak to me.

Consider for a moment the idea that God is sovereign. This idea communicates something about the nature of God. To say that God is sovereign is to understand that God is in control of all events. In addition, God's control is grounded in God possessing perfect power and perfect wisdom; God *knows* exactly what to do and God has *the ability* to bring it to pass. It is because God is sovereign that God can work all things together for our good. Scripture describes God's sovereignty in different ways by calling God a king who rules righteously, a warrior who fights on behalf of his people, one who controls the winds and the waves, etc. Praying in light of the idea that God is sovereign would go something like this:

God, I know that you are in control of the events of my life. For you are God and there is no other, you are God and

6. Karl Barth, *Evangelical Theology: An Introduction*, trans. G. Farley (Grand Rapids, MI: Eerdmans, 1979), 171.

there is no one like you (Is. 46:9). You ride on the wings of wind (Ps. 18:10); you hide me beneath the shelter of your wings (Ps. 61:4); you protect me from the storm; for you, O Lord, calm the storm and bring peace to my life. I trust that you are working all things together for my good (Rom. 8:28) because I know that there is nothing outside of your control. For the eyes of the Lord survey the earth (2 Chron. 16:9; Zech. 4:10) and there is nothing hidden from them. Lord, you know my future, there is nothing hidden from your sight; you see farther than I can and I know that you will do what is right for me.

Notice that scriptural ideas run throughout the prayer and fill out the idea that God is sovereign. We know what it means to say that God is sovereign by studying God. To pray this way--to have one's prayer filled with scriptural ideas about God--requires that the person engage in theology. The scriptural ideas fill out our portrait of God so that we can know not only that God is sovereign but also what that means. We are getting to know God.

I hope this example illustrates how praying our theology helps us construct a picture of the God to whom we are praying. We serve a personal God who eternally exists as Father, Son and Holy Spirit. Since prayer is just simply talking to God, we learn to talk to God by getting to know something about God. The more we get to know God, the more we cultivate intimacy with God. Praying our theology helps us come to know something about God.

Secondly, *we dialogue with God by listening to the voice of the Spirit speaking to our hearts*. When I suggest that we listen to the Spirit's voice, I do not mean that we should wait to hear some audible voice. The Spirit speaks in a variety of ways. In an important sense, the Spirit talks to us through the scriptures giving us a portrait of the Father and the Son which forms our theology. In addition, when we pray our theology, the Spirit can speak to us by reminding us of what God has done or helping us to see how God is working. Praying through the idea that God is sovereign may help us to know that God is working even when we cannot see what God is doing. The Spirit may remind us that God will bring us through a particular trial because God is sovereign and we need simply to trust in God. Conversely, the Spirit may convict us and suggest that we need to allow God to exercise sovereignty over our lives by surrendering certain areas to him.

As the Spirit convicts us or reminds us of God's work, our prayer becomes a true dialogue with God speaking to us even as we talk to him. How does this happen? Sometimes the Spirit speaks to us by giving us strong impressions about ourselves. As we pray, "God I know you are in charge of my situation," the Spirit may impress upon our minds the idea or thought that God has not left us but is always with us. This is one way the Spirit can bring comfort. The Spirit can also take us to a passage of scripture that may address our particular situation. He may bring to mind Paul's declaration that nothing can separate us from the love of God (Rom. 8:37-39) or Jesus' words "Lo, I am with you always" (Matt. 28:20). A third way the Spirit speaks is by helping to make connections between different ideas or to find a meaning to a passage of scripture that before was hidden from us. Remember the example I gave of singing the chorus based on Isaiah 6 and Isaiah's vision of God. As I sang that song, the Spirit helped me to begin to make connections between the words of the song, Isaiah's text and my own desires for God's kingdom to be established. In all of these ways and more, the Spirit speaks to us as we pray and inflames our desires for God.

A Tale of Two Loves: Passion and a Loving Disposition

In this chapter I have discussed how love for God inflames the believer by creating holy passions for God. But these holy passions should be distinguished from a constant loving disposition that comes over time. As a result of their emotional intensity, sometimes people mistake passions for a loving disposition. Passions tend to be strong desires grounded upon an attraction to someone or something whereas a loving disposition points toward a character state or condition that causes one to cleave to another over the long haul. In English, we use the word love to refer both to passions and a loving disposition, but these two should be kept separate. When Shakespeare declares that love is "an ever-fixed mark" he is referring to a constant disposition that a person has to cling to his beloved. Passions provide an important ingredient in any loving relationship, but if that relationship is going to last, it must include more than mere passions. Since pursuing holiness is a lifelong journey of uniting ourselves to Christ in ever increasing degrees, we need determination and stamina to go the distance. This determination begins with rekindling holy passions for God and is consummated when those passions solidify into a constant loving disposition.

We can get a clearer understanding of the difference between passions and a loving disposition by returning to the relationship between a husband and a wife. Any romance between two persons usually begins with some sort of attraction. We are initially attracted to him or her for a variety of reasons. A part of the attraction is physical in that we find the person's facial features, hair style and bodily shapes and curves appealing. Another part of our attraction is caused by the individual's personality, whether the person is funny or serious, shares our likes or dislikes, etc. Over time our attraction can become stronger or weaker as we learn more about the individual. If the attraction grows, it can form a passion just for this one person that eventually leads to asking for his or her hand in marriage. Once we move into the marital state, we must learn to combine passion for our mate with actions giving expression to that passion. For example, we take our spouse out for dinner, buy him/her nice clothes, take out the trash, mow the lawn, wash the dishes, share our hopes and dreams with him/her and a host of other actions that express how committed we are. When we combine passionate commitment with actions, we create a permanent loving disposition that causes us to cleave to that person over and above anyone else. Even when passions erupt in physical attraction for someone else, which they can do from time to time, this loving disposition solidifies our commitment to the person and forms the covenantal framework for marriage.

The fact of divorce tells us that couples do not always stabilize their passion for one another. This is especially the case with so-called no fault divorces where spouses simply decide they can no longer live with one another. They "fall out of love" with one another in part because they fail to turn their initial passion for one another into a constant loving disposition. At the end of the day, passion–even holy passion–is fleeting, here one moment gone the next. While setting our hearts on fire for God helps keep us on the path of holiness, we must make that passion permanent. As we cultivate our passion for God and turn it into a loving disposition, we find ourselves running in such a way as to obtain the prize.

Chapter 8
Fostering a Holy Life

But the fruit of the Spirit is love, joy, peace, longsuffering,
kindness, goodness, faithfulness, gentleness, self-control.
Against such there is no law. And those who are Christ's
have crucified the flesh with its passions and desires.
If we live in the Spirit, let us also walk in the Spirit.

(Gal. 5:22-25; NKJV)

The title of this chapter may strike the reader as odd since the previous chapter seems to cover at least some of the same ground. Although this chapter continues with the idea of practicing the presence of God in worship, I want to weave together some themes that I have discussed but not yet developed fully. The previous chapter was devoted to sustaining our pursuit of holiness by cultivating a passion for God that more closely unites us to the eternal bridegroom. Moreover, I suggested that this can occur through worship and prayer. As we worship God in song and seek intimacy in prayer, our hearts are set aflame by the Spirit of God, which motivates us to pursue holiness. In this chapter, we need to explore how love of neighbor also aids the pursuit of holiness even in the midst of the most ordinary tasks like clearing some brush or serving a meal in Jesus' name. Whether we realize it or not, these tasks performed in worship to God and in service to neighbor have transforming effects that conform us to Christ and so make us holy. To see this more clearly, we need

183

to draw on our discussions of calling and community in chapter four noting how they relate to the development of the fruit of the Spirit without which we could not be holy.

Developing the Fruit of the Spirit

I have often asked my students how they acquire the fruit of the Spirit. Does this fruit simply appear in one's life one day? Does God simply decide, "Today, I will make this person gentle because she's asked me enough?" The first response usually comes in this way: "Yes, God does simply decide. If you ask God in prayer, he will give you the fruit of the Spirit in the same way that God decides to heal." This first response does not take into account the difference between God healing the physical body and God healing the whole person body and soul. God can cure a physical disease in a moment in the same way that some medications can cure physical diseases, but God cannot make us holy in a moment. Why? Because to do so would be to violate the role we play in salvation through our free choice. Paul tells us that we must keep in step with the Spirit which implies that we must choose to cooperate with the Spirit's work in our lives. When we pray and ask God to help us become a gentle person, we are asking the Spirit to empower us to put feet to our prayers and do gentle deeds in and among the community of faith and the larger community to which we belong. As James suggests, faith without works is dead (James 2:14-26). Or, to put it in Paul's words, "the only thing that counts is faith *working* through love" (Gal. 5:6). Only the faith that seeks to keep in step with the Spirit by performing good works of love for neighbor develops the fruit of gentleness, kindness, etc.

Recall that when I dealt with election and predestination in chapter five, I suggested that what we believe about predestination affects how we think God works in the world, especially in God's dealing with humans. If we think that God predestines people in such a way as to work in concert with their free choice, then we should assume that God always works this way. God does not allow us the freedom to choose Christ initially and then prevent us from choosing otherwise. We always remain free to choose or not to choose Christ and that extends to the choices that go hand in hand with keeping in step with the Spirit.

A second objection usually emerges at this point: "When I ask God to give me the fruit of the Spirit, how is that violating my free choice?" I think once we see how we develop the fruit of the Spirit, the answer to this question will become clear. Let me begin by pointing out that when Paul lists various fruit of the Spirit he is simply describing a list of virtues or character traits (see diagram).[1] In fact, Paul has several places where he provides these lists for his readers (2 Cor. 6:6; Gal. 5:22-23; Phil. 4:8; Col. 3:12). As Gordon Fee notes, Paul calls these character traits "fruits of the Spirit" because he wants to highlight the fact that they grow in believers from the Spirit's work.[2] Consequently, it would be

---

1. See Dunn, *Theology of Paul*, 662-5; and Fee, *God's Empowering Presence*, 443-54.

2. Ibid., 443-44.

wrong to draw the conclusion that believers should remain passive and simply ask the Spirit to suddenly produce this fruit. Instead, Paul's admonition that his readers must walk with the Spirit (Gal. 5:25) implies that this fruit grows gradually as the believer cooperates with the work of the Spirit. This should be enough to convince us that we must choose to cooperate with the Spirit every step of the journey, but there are other reasons as well.

Gal. 5.22-23	Col. 3.12	Cor. 6.6	Phil. 4.8
love	compassion	purity	truth
patience	lowliness	patience	honor
goodness	patience	love	pure
gentleness	kindness	kindness	lovely
faithfulness	meekness	knowledge	graciousness
peace		truthful speech	just
kindness			
self-control			

Let me pick up on the point that what Paul describes as "fruit" we normally call character traits or virtues. When we think of virtues or character traits we should see them as life skills. A skill is something that must be developed over time. A person may have the natural talent to play baseball, but he still must develop the skills that go along with playing the game. The baseball player develops these skills gradually as he practices and practices. I could make the same point about

186

all kinds of activities like singing, carpentry, cooking, public speaking, playing an instrument, etc. If we are going to flourish in these activities, that is, if we are going to perform them well, then we must develop a set a skills through practice that goes along with them. Skills, like eye-hand coordination when swinging a baseball bat, help *perfect* or *complete* the baseball player, causing him to play the game well. Sandy Koufax pitched the perfect game because he first developed the skills that go hand in hand with pitching. Without those skills, Koufax would never have learned to control his fast ball and, consequently, would never have pitched the perfect game. The important point about skills is that they complete or perfect the person by helping him develop his complete potential. Flourishing comes after the skills have been fully developed. What Paul is describing for us is a set of life skills that goes hand in hand with living well.

Like any other set of skills, these skills only come through practice, in particular, the practice of living the Christian life as the Spirit empowers, guides and directs. As I often say to my students, no one becomes gentle without performing gentle actions over and over again in the same way that no one becomes a good baseball player without swinging a bat or throwing a baseball over and over again. Consequently, God does not instantly make us gentle or kind, but empowers us daily to perform gentle actions such that over the course of our lives we become gentle and kind. This is how God works in concert with our free choices to make us holy over the course of our lives.

For Paul, an individual takes on the character of God by developing these life skills. The person who fully develops all of the fruit of the Spirit no longer needs the law because that person now possesses the very character of Christ in his life. One could suggest that the law is written upon the heart of the person who fully possesses the fruit of the Spirit. In the same way that Sandy Koufax does by nature what the rules of pitching require because he has acquired the skills of pitching so Christians do by nature what the law of God requires because they have the fruit.

What I am pushing us toward is a view of the Christian life that sees developing holiness and being transformed as the equivalent of putting on the character of Christ. When we talk about someone having "character" we usually mean that the person has a set of habits or ingrained dispositions. Habits in the way I'm using the term is simply another word for skills. A habit refers to a pattern of behavior that results either from an addiction to some chemical or from doing the same activity over and over again. The habit of smoking is a result of the addictive nature of nicotine. However, the habit of lying is a result of someone telling one lie after another such that a pattern of behavior eventually develops. If a person lies enough times, he predisposes himself to tell another lie. That is, he cultivates an ingrained disposition to lie. Once the person has a habit or an ingrained disposition, we could now say that he has the character of a liar. While I have described two bad habits, the same is true of any good habits that we want to develop. When Paul calls gentleness a fruit of the

Spirit, he means that gentleness is a habit or ingrained disposition that results from our working in cooperation with the Spirit. Once we have the habit in place, we can say that we have put on that characteristic of Christ. The goal of the Christian life is to put on the character of Christ by developing within us the habits that predispose us to act in the way that Christ acted.

Imitating Christ

Putting on the character of Christ involves a transformation from one set of character traits to another set of character traits. What we are attempting to do is cultivate a pattern of thinking and behaving that is reflective of Christ's own life. We want to be like Jesus. Theologians have described this approach to holiness as an imitation of Christ because it suggests that we are striving to imitate or be like Christ in all that we say and do. One of the ways we seek to imitate Christ is by looking at his teachings and actions. What did Christ say about loving our neighbor? How did he treat people? How did he show compassion? How did he display love? In what way did he humble himself? Answering these questions requires a close examination of the Gospels because that is where we find the story of Jesus. By examining the story of Jesus we can begin to glimpse an alternative way of living in the world. Jesus teaches us how to live as members of an alternative reality, the kingdom of God. To put it in another way, Jesus is showing us a new kind of humanity where we relate to one another and to God in righteous ways.

He is revealing to us what it means to be truly human. It is a new way of living that necessitates developing a new set of character traits.

If we return to the Sermon on the Mount for a moment, we can see what I mean by a new way of living in the world. Like Moses before him, Jesus is handing out the law of God. However, there is an important difference. Jesus is not simply receiving the law from God and then communicating it to the people. Instead, he is giving the law of God. He is not simply a new Moses, he is more than Moses. Throughout the beginning of the sermon, Jesus repeatedly says, "you have heard it said... but I say to you" (Matt. 5:21-22, 27-28, 31-32, 33-34, 38-39, 43-44) to emphasize the fact that he is teaching a different kind of life than even the law of Moses taught. This new kind of life does not do away with the law of Moses; instead, it moves beyond the law. By the time Jesus gets to the end of the first part of the sermon, he lays out the bombshell, "be perfect as your Father in heaven is perfect" (Matt. 5:48). Dietrich Bonhoeffer calls this command the "extraordinary" because it points us to a life of undivided love where we are called to reflect God's love as exemplified in Christ's willingness to love to the uttermost by dying on a cross. When one reads this passage, one can understand why Dietrich Bonhoeffer titles his examination of the Sermon on the Mount, *The Cost of Discipleship*. Christ is teaching a new way of living that is nothing less than the "extraordinary."[3]

---

3. D. Bonhoeffer, *Cost of Discipleship*, 171.

A closer look at the Sermon helps us to decipher how Jesus proposes that we go beyond the law. Jesus is not as interested in external behavior as he is in internal behavior.[4] He is really interested in getting us to cultivate internal attitudes or mind sets. For example, he wants us to be poor in spirit (humble), mourners (those who compassionately weep with others in their tragedies) meek (gentle), peacemakers (just), merciful, etc. (Matt. 5:1-12). All of these traits relate to internal attitudes or habits that we must develop. The person who possesses the qualities of meekness, mercy and peacemaking will also have the self control not to lash out in anger and curse his brother or sister (Matt. 5:21-26). Jesus is asking us to reshape our lives by a new set of character traits that turn out to be remarkably similar to Paul's list of the fruits of the Spirit. By these new character traits or habits, Jesus shows us how to fulfill the law.

Let me now make a comment that may at first seem controversial. While it is very important to examine the life and teachings of Christ in order to put on the character of Christ, if this is all we do, we will not have done enough. It is not that the teachings of Christ are deficient in any way; they are not. Nor is it that the teachings of Christ are no longer relevant; they are. Instead, the problem has to do with the distance between us and Christ. We live in the twenty-first century while Christ lived in the first century. The difficulties

---

4. See Ellen T. Charry, *By the Renewing of Your Minds: The Pastoral Function of Christian Doctrine* (New York, NY: Oxford University Press, 1997), 61-83, who makes this point.

we face are not always the same as those Christ faced. What we find ourselves trying to do is apply Christ's actions and teachings to a variety of situations that Christ himself never faced. Jesus did not deal with modern entertainment, owning and driving a car, investing, consumer credit, In vitro fertilization, cloning, etc. Of course, we can draw implications from Jesus' words and actions to deal with these issues, but we should recognize what we're doing. Jesus was never in a situation where it was either lie and protect the Jews in your basement or tell the truth and give up the Jews to the Nazi's knowing that they will be murdered. He never asked the question of whether driving a Mercedes was too much. There was never a question about investing in a business with morally questionable practices or investing in an IRA that has shares in a company with questionable moral practices. He did not wonder whether a defense attorney should attack and impugn the testimony of an honest witness in the service of defending his client. I could go on and on with the modern moral dilemmas we face, but I hope that the point has been made. As important as the teachings and life of Christ are, we also need to recognize that they simply do not cover every situation we will encounter as twenty-first century Christians.

How do we respond to this difficulty? We must become people of character. Our actions not only shape our character, they also come from it. If we walk with the Spirit, we will be constructing the character of Christ in us. The person with a kind disposition will have an easier time discerning what the kind response to a situation must be than the person who is prone to angry outbursts. The one who has angry outbursts will be more likely to engage in a rash action that he will regret. His anger may blind him to the truth as to his proper response. The person with a habit of truth-telling will have an easier time figuring out what it means to tell the truth in a particular situation than the person who has the habit of lying. The individual who practices the just treatment of other persons will be better situated to consider what the just action must be than the individual who constantly treats people unjustly. By keeping in step with the Spirit, slowly over the course of our lives we become people of character, which will guide us in our actions and help us to discover the truth as to what we should do.

There is a second difficulty given the distance between us and Christ that can be easily seen in a story commonly told in sermons. The story is of a little child who was afraid of the dark and could not sleep. Initially, the father went into the room of the child and indicated that he and the child's mother were in the next room so there was no need to be afraid. Of course, the child didn't buy it, so the father next said, "Jesus is here with you." The reply was, "I need Jesus with skin on him." The interesting side of this story is the implication that there is a great distance between Jesus and us. We cannot see or listen to Jesus anymore and the child, to his credit, recognized this fact. The picture we have of Christ in the New Testament does not cover every situation even he dealt with. In addition, Christ is no longer present to show us how to handle situations. The importance of this for our discussion is that Jesus is not a *living* example to us that we can watch. When I say living example, I don't mean to imply that Jesus is not alive. I'm simply asserting that Jesus is no longer walking around on planet earth teaching us and providing an example of character. What is implicit in the child's comment is that we need a *living* Jesus who will serve as an example for us. We need a person or group of persons who model Christian behavior and with whom we can discuss all of the dilemmas we face. In short, we need the church.

The Church as a Community of Character

All of this talk about the need to cultivate the character of Christ in our lives leads us toward the community of disciples to which we must belong. When we consider that we form our character as we develop a set of skills or habits, we can begin to see the need for other people in our lives.[5] The formation of character requires other people for at least three reasons. First, the old saying that character is caught not taught suggests to us that we learn what good character is from other people. Character can only be caught when there is someone with good character around to catch it from. Second, we need other people with whom we can practice our righteous acts. To do a kind action requires another human being who is the recipient of our kindness. Third, we need people who will help us discover exactly where sin blinds us. We are all blind to the truth in some way and none of us recognizes all the ways in which we are blind. These three

---

5. I have drawn some of the ideas for this section from Stanley Hauerwas's discussions of the church. See his *The Peaceable Kingdom: A Primer in Christian Ethics* (Notre Dame: University of Notre Dame Press, 1983), 96ff; and *A Community of Character: Toward a Constructive Christian Social Ethic* (Notre Dame: University of Notre Dame Press, 1981), 111ff.

194

reasons tell us how important the kind of community is to which we belong. One of the reasons why God "calls" believers to be a part of his body is that body life produces disciples. We learn how to put on Christ as we participate in body life. It is in the body of Christ that we find good examples of righteous character, the opportunity to perform righteous deeds and the insight into our own behavior that we need.

Let me deal with the first and last points together. It is important to surround ourselves with people of character who can serve as guides in our attempt to learn how to love our neighbors. We take on character traits primarily by imitating those around us. As we watch how others act, we mimic their actions in our lives. In this way, character slowly forms in us because we gradually sometimes imperceptibly conform our lives to those around us. I can recall moments in my childhood where I "caught" from my parents and others in my church what it means to be Christlike. I remember when my mother allowed my cousin to move in with us. As a teenager caught up in his own world, I protested this decision vigorously. I did not like my cousin and now I was being asked to live with her. I will never forget my mother's response. "Son, she needs our help. What do you want me to do? Turn her away?" In that brief moment, I saw compassion in action and it knocked me out of my own selfishness. Although I did not realize it at the time, I had just "caught" some character from my mother.

There is another moment in the life of my church that I will not forget. At the time, our church was collectively deciding whether to split into two churches. It was a horrible time for the congregation. Most persons were forced to choose a side. Families were divided. One night we were having a church-wide discussion about the issue. The appropriate church officials were present to help the church decide whether a split was absolutely necessary. During that meeting one woman, who rarely voiced her opinion publicly, stood up and said that she was willing to leave rather than see the church split. As she spoke, I saw her courage and humility in action. Here was a woman who would rather give up her place in a church where she had been for ten or more years if it brought peace. She helped me catch the virtues of courage and humility by her actions.

While no one has perfect character, it is important to belong to a community of character. Moreover, it is important to belong to a community that reflects the kind of character we want to develop. Of course, we don't wait to belong to the church. When we become a Christian, we become a part of the church. As the body of Christ, the church is a community of disciples actively seeking to be led by the Spirit and to put on the character of Christ. This is the community to which we belong, which means that we must be a part of a local church. By seeking to be a community of character, the church fosters an environment where Christians learn what it means to be Christian.

To become a part of a community of disciples is to open oneself up to their influence as well as to exercise influence upon them. This is the essence of accountability. The closer we get to other people, the more they know about us.

Growing up in the U.S., I realize how uncomfortable this is for us. We prefer the comfort of our privacy to the discomfort of learning to relate to others. Privacy is always more comfortable because one is never challenged to grow and change. However, to become all that we can be in Christ, we need to hear the voice of the Spirit speaking through our fellow believers. This is not about one group having authority over us; rather, as I said, it is about being open to the influence of others. When the church becomes a place where believers influence and are influenced by one another, it begins to be a place where healing and wholeness can occur.

Many Christians have a go-it-alone mentality. They believe that they can live their Christian lives just fine by attending church on Sunday morning and not being invested in a community. What these Christians fail to realize is how blind they are to their own self-destructive behavior. In the midst of the give and take of community life, we learn about ourselves and our weaknesses. God also uses us to teach others about themselves. When faced with a fellow Christian who gives until it hurts, the Spirit might challenge us to look at our own selfishness. As one man watches another treating his wife with care and concern, he might be led to see how neglectful he has been. Whenever we live a solitary Christian life, we diminish ourselves and become anemic Christians who don't grow in grace.

Finally, the fruit of the Spirit must be practiced. The practice of kindness, gentleness, etc., occurs in and through the community of disciples to which we belong. A second place where we practice the fruit of the Spirit is in the world to which we are called to minister. While I have spent much of this chapter discussing the role of the church in forming our character, this should not be taken as a lack of concern for neighbor love outside of the church. The church cannot be God's community unless, like God, it remains open to the world. This means that our local churches must extend God's hand to all those around and invite them to be a part of their fellowship. Practicing the fruit of the Spirit involves seeking to form Christ's character in all of our actions both within the community of faith and as an extension of the community of faith.

Throughout the entire process of learning to love our neighbor the Spirit is at work. Sometimes, the Spirit prompts us in our hearts to respond to another person with an act of kindness. At other times, the Spirit uses a fellow believer to challenge our views about some issue. However, the primary point we need to see is that the Spirit works in our lives within the context of the body and not apart from it. By responding to the Spirit's voice, we cooperative with God's effort to construct the character of Christ in us and so heal us of the self-destructive patterns of behavior that have dominated our lives.

The Transforming Power of Neighbor Love

I have spent most of this chapter explaining how it is that we may be transformed by loving our neighbor. The practice of neighbor love is an activity that requires change. We must repent of sinful patterns of behaving and thinking that prevent us from fully expressing neighbor love. In this respect, there is little difference between Paul's desire for us to develop the fruit of the Spirit and Christ's call to be his disciples. Both the fruit of the Spirit and the characteristics of Christ's disciples deal with the development of life skills or habits reflective of a new humanity. Christ wants us to take on his own righteous character, which itself exemplifies the character of God. For Paul, we put on the righteous character of Christ by walking in the Spirit over the course of our lives. As we practice neighbor love, we change and conform our lives to Christ.

Constructing Christ's character within us is about the gradual movement from one kind of life to another. We make this journey one choice at a time. By choosing to cooperate with the Spirit, we slowly develop righteous habits that bring about our transformation. This transforming journey is about God slowly healing us and enabling us to fulfil our complete potential as members of his new humanity. We cannot forget that this movement from one kind of life to another is good for us because it enables us to be all that we were intended to be.

Another way of describing the transforming journey of neighbor love is practicing the presence of God.[6] To practice the presence of God is to view each action, each choice as directed toward God. Even the choices to love our neighbor can and should be directed toward God. When we view our actions in this way, we are seeing them as a form of worship. As Paul admonishes us, we must present our bodies as living

---

6. See Brother Lawrence of the Resurrection, *The Practice of the Presence of God*, trans. with an intro. J. J. Delaney (New York, NY: Doubleday, 1996).

sacrifices, which itself is a spiritual act of worship (Rom. 12:1). Becoming a living sacrifice means pouring out one's life for others. This is what Christ did and this is what neighbor love demands. Our worship to God occurs in the midst of everyday tasks where we seek to pour out ourselves in service to others. How is this any different from James' claim that pure religion is visiting the orphans and widows and keeping oneself unstained from the world (Jas. 1:27)? Whether you call it pure religion or true worship, it is practicing the presence of God by seeing each choice to love a neighbor as a choice to love God.

Notice what else Paul says. He follows up his admonition to present oneself as a living sacrifice with the command to be transformed by renewing our minds (Rom. 12:2). How do we transform our patterns of thinking and behaving? Precisely by engaging in the kind of behavior appropriate to a living sacrifice. When we choose to pour ourselves out in service to neighbor, we are transformed. Serving a cup of water in Jesus' name helps us to become kind because it involves a conscious choice to engage in an act of kindness. We are being made holy by these actions. That is, God is pouring out his own life into us as we choose to cooperate with the Spirit in performing acts of kindness, gentleness, etc. As we worship the Lord by serving our neighbor, we united ourselves more closely with the Lord of glory who did not consider equality with God something to be grasped. This new way of life that teaches us to be human also becomes the means of our achieving wholeness.

The community of Christ's disciples to which we belong models the new way of living in the world for us and becomes the place where we practice the presence of God. The church is the temple of the Spirit because it is the place where the Spirit is fashioning a new people who reflect the beauty of God in their lives. We practice holiness as we seek to relate righteously to fellow believers. Likewise, we learn about holiness as we watch our fellow believers relate righteously to one another. Since every believer is still on the journey toward perfection, we encourage holiness in one another through forgiveness, consolation and, sometimes, confrontation. In all these ways, the community seeks to model what behavior should be like in the kingdom of God.

The church also has a mission to bring this new way of living to the world. This means that acts of kindness should not be reserved for fellow believers. Believers do not separate themselves from the world by sealing themselves off from others. We separate ourselves from the world by engaging in a form of behavior that the world does and does not recognize. The world does not recognize the behavior of the church because this behavior should reflect the character of God. Instead of contributing to the destructive patterns of behaving that make up the world, believers should seek to work against those patterns of behavior by modeling Christ. Moreover, if Christ shows us what it means to be human, when the church models Christ, the world will recognize itself. The world will see in Christians not what it is, a place where the slavery of sinful thinking and behaving dominate, but what it could be and should be. It will recognize in

Christians what it means to lift up one's fellow human beings rather than beat them down. It will see in Christians what it means to love and be loved. In short, the world will gain a glimpse of what it means to be human in the community of Christ's disciples. This is how the church continues God's mission in the world.

My argument has now come full circle. Our worship to God is expressed both in terms of love for God and love for neighbor. In its fullest sense, worship is seeing God as the only one who can help us reach our complete potential. From the beginning, we were designed to be in relationship with God and to express that relationship by righteously relating to one another. True love for God *is* love for neighbor and true love for neighbor *is* love for God. This is what holiness is and what holiness does. Our pursuit of holiness is a quest to be transformed by the triune God of grace so that we can reflect this God in all that we say and do. In the end, there should be no separation between loving God and loving neighbor because both are a part of the same fabric of healthy, whole and holy relations.

Chapter 9
A View from the End

Then I saw a new heaven and a new earth;
for the first heaven and the first earth had passed away,
and the sea was no more. And I saw the holy city,
new Jerusalem coming down out of heaven from God,
prepared as a bride adorned for her husband;
and I heard a loud voice from the throne saying,
"Behold, the dwelling of God is with men.
He will dwell with them, and they shall be his people,
and God himself will be with them;
he will wipe away every tear from their eyes,
and death shall be no more, neither shall there be mourning
nor crying nor pain any more, for the former things have passed away
(Rev. 21:1-6; *RSV*)

As a conclusion to this brief look at holiness, I want us to consider the nature of the end of all things. One could sum up the end with the one word I mentioned previously: shalom. Shalom is the condition in which peace and justice embrace in the harmony of all things. Isaiah captures shalom in the image of a lion lying down with a lamb to bring together God's purpose for humanity and God's purpose for the universe. God's shalom is God's bringing into harmonious relation all things under himself, and this happens through Christ in the

Spirit. When humans attain the beauty of perfection, they attain shalom, peace within themselves, peace with one another, peace with creation and peace with God. This is the ultimate purpose of holy living, to be made one with God and thus to be at peace.

When we arrive at shalom, we arrive at perfection. However, the kind of perfection I have in mind may be better described by the word completion. It is not an absolute perfection because only God can be absolutely perfect. Instead, we become perfect in the sense that we have completely realized our potential as human beings such that we lack nothing. To lack nothing is to be complete. I did not say that we needed nothing because we always will need God to support us even in our perfected state. Since, as humans, our very existence remains dependent upon God, a part of arriving at perfection where we lack nothing involves entering into full or complete participation in God. To lack a relationship with God is to lack something and thus to remain incomplete.

A Picture of Shalom

Shalom is what Cornelius Plantinga identifies as "the way things ought to be." Plantinga goes on to define shalom in this way:

The webbing together of God, humans, and all creation in justice, fulfillment, and delight is what the Hebrew prophets call *shalom*. We call it peace, but it means far more than mere peace of mind or a cease-fire between enemies. In the Bible, shalom means *universal flourishing, wholeness, and delight*—a rich state of affairs in which natural needs are satisfied and natural gifts fruitfully employed, a state of affairs that inspires joyful wonder as its Creator and Savior opens doors and welcomes the creatures in whom he delights.[1]

The wholeness or flourishing that is shalom is the way the world was intended to be before things got messed up. A close look at the first chapter of Genesis tells us as much. When we read Genesis 1 carefully, we see a world in balance and harmony. God is creating all things by bringing order to the chaos. After the opening verse, the writer states, "And the earth was formless and void and darkness was upon the face of the deep" (Gen. 1:2). The terms formless and void point to a hideous abyss or desert waste. Out of this shapeless and lifeless state, God begins to weave together a beautiful world where everything has its proper place. It is no mistake that the writer uses the verb "to separate" five times in the course of the opening chapter (Gen. 1:4, 6, 7, 14, 18). When God creates he brings symmetry and structure by separating things out from one another. Every object in creation has its role to play in the world, the light, the waters, the dry land, the vegetation, the animals, all take their rightful place. It is a world at peace where everything flourishes through harmonious balance. It is a picture of shalom.

---

1. Plantinga, *Not the Way It's Supposed to Be*, 10.

Shalom is what the Old Testament prophets long for. When Jeremiah looks at the nation of Israel, he finds that her sinfulness has negated God's own shalom. "I beheld the earth, and indeed it was without form and void; and the heavens, they had no light" (Jer. 4:23). What Jeremiah sees is literally uncreation, a reversal of God's creative work. This is what sin does. It disintegrates the wholeness of God's creation. The disease of sin produces a world that constantly vandalizes God's shalom.[2] It is the cascading effect of no longer living in fellowship with God. When Jeremiah looks at Israel he laments the fact that the chaos and disorder out of which God made the world has now returned. Through Jeremiah, we see how sin pollutes the entire created order by breaking down relationships in fundamental ways. There is no peace, only confusion and disorder, fighting and disintegration. Into this state of affairs, Isaiah announces that "unto us a child is born... and his name will be called Wonderful, Counselor, Mighty God, Everlasting Father" and finally, "Prince of Peace" or shalom (Is. 9:6). This heir to David's throne will usher in God's righteous reign of shalom once again.

Drawing on the establishment of shalom, Paul makes it clear that Christ is "our peace" because in his life and death, he is restoring a wholeness of relations among people (Eph. 2:14-18). Where there is currently division and strife resulting from vandalism of God's shalom, Christ is preaching peace to those far off and those near with the express aim of creating a

---

2. Ibid., 7ff.

new humanity. Although Christ has won this peace through his death on the cross, it must be actualized in the world. Paul sees this occurring by means of the Spirit because it is the Spirit who opens up the way to the Father (Eph. 2:18). The full realization of God's shalom will come as the Spirit unites all persons in Christ to the glory of the Father.

When we turn to the book of Revelation, we discover that the story ends with the restoration of God's shalom through the triumphant Lamb. As the seventh angel announces after he blows his trumpet, "the kingdoms of this world have become the kingdoms of our Lord and of His Christ" (Rev. 11:15). The image of Jesus as the Lamb slain in Revelation points toward the death of Christ. The one who has conquered is none other than the one who suffered and died (Rev. 5:6). John, like Paul, suggests that the victory has yet to be realized fully. The Lamb who was slain must return on a white horse to establish God's righteous reign of peace once and for all. John sees Christ, the spotless Lamb returning on a white horse as the heavens open (Rev. 19:11). The robe of Christ is dipped in blood suggesting a reference to his death even as he now comes in power and glory. He is described as "faithful and true" because he is the Word of God who was faithful and is the Truth. As Richard Baukcham notes, Christ is coming as the Truth to dispel the lies of the beast.[3] All of the

---

3. R. Bauckham, *The Theology of the Book of Revelation* (Cambridge: Cambridge University Press, 1993), 104-06.

deception and blindness brought on by sin will be removed one day as Christ comes in his glory.

Revelation concludes with a vivid contrast between two ways of living, the New Jerusalem and Babylon.[4] For John, the city of Babylon was Rome in her economic might (Rev. 17 and 18). Because of her economic prosperity, Rome was as attractive and deceptive as any harlot. She dominated the world and sought to seduce all peoples through her wealth and splendor. During John's day, Rome heralded itself as the empire who brought peace. One of the slogans of the time was *Pax Romana* (Roman Peace), which referred to the peace and prosperity brought about by Rome. To John, this slogan was no more than a piece of propaganda for a way of life that really brought destruction and death.[5] In the end, Babylon is a symbol for the destructive nature of life outside of God. As the opposite of God's shalom, Babylon exemplifies the fruit of the disease of sin, which John describes as the plagues of death, mourning and famine (Rev. 18:8). The outcome of this way of life is certain.

The New Jerusalem is the divine alternative to Babylon. It is portrayed as a place, a people and a presence.[6] When John

---

4. Ibid., 126ff; see also R. Bauckham, *The Climax of Prophecy: Studies on the Book of Revelation* (Edinburgh: T & T Clark, 1993), 338; and R. Hollis Gause, *Revelation: God's Stamp of Sovereignty on History* (Cleveland, TN: Pathway Press, 1983), 219.

5. Bauckham, *Climax of Prophecy*, 347.

6. Bauckham, *Theology of Revelation*, 132.

sees it coming down from heaven, he first describes it as a bride (Rev. 21:1-2). This description is immediately followed with an announcement that the dwelling or tabernacle of God will now be with humanity (Rev. 1:3). In these three verses, John depicts the New Jerusalem as a people (the bride) and as the presence of God. No temple exists in this new city because God's presence will permeate every part of it. In addition, there is no crying or weeping, no pain or death. Instead, God's own life will flow out from his throne and enliven all things (Rev. 22:1). Like a divine environmental clean-up program, God's presence will immediately remove all the spiritual pollution and hazardous waste left over from the world's sinful state. Finally, God's presence will produce a new paradise or a new creation. It is the New Jerusalem (shalom), the city of peace, God's final peace.

One does not have to read John's description very closely to see that the New Jerusalem both as the bride of Christ and the city of peace will possess unsurpassed beauty. This beauty is to be a reflection of the glory of God. Richard Bauckham points out the connection between John's description of God as being like jasper (4:3) and the New Jerusalem as having a light like a jasper stone (21:11). j states, "John probably means that the whole city... shines with the reflected glory of God himself."[7] Just as the tabernacle and the temple, the New

---

7. Ibid., 134.

Jerusalem is set apart unto God by her splendor and radiance. The shalom that characterizes it will give rise to this beauty. It is the beauty of God's own perfection reflected in the holiness of the bride as well as the architecture of the city itself. As the place of God's presence, the New Jerusalem shows us how shalom and perfection go hand in hand. God's perfection gives rise to beauty, harmony and order. It is the beauty of God's own life, and he extends this beauty to his creation. When we finally arrive at the New Jerusalem, when we finally become the New Jerusalem we will reach our complete potential in the beauty of his holiness.

Some Blessings to Keep Before Us

My desire in this book was to evoke a vision of holiness that would incite us to live a life that is pure and undefiled before the Lord. I leave it up to the reader to judge the success of this project. However, I would like to conclude with a brief mention of the blessings that result from a holy life; yes there are blessings, but they may turn out to differ from first impressions. These blessings are not primarily associated with material possessions or the accumulation of what I have called *worldly* things. That is, those things affiliated with a way of life contrary to the Christian vision. These are not to be identified with the allure of Babylon. Rather, the blessings of holiness are bound up with its ultimate purpose or end: God himself. We often mistakenly perceive these blessings as the end itself and so seek after them rather than their author.

This mistaken perception attaches to a central theme running throughout scripture which is addressed primarily by the first commandment: "you shall have no other gods before me." Perceiving God as merely the means to some greater blessing violates that commandment. God must always be the end, the ultimate point of all we do, and never the means.

If God is the end and the blessings of holiness are bound up with that end then an individual receives those blessings in proportion to her sharing God's own life. To put it simply, the more one participates in God the closer to God one becomes and the more one shares God's life. Holiness has its aim in a participation in the divine life of God. Its rewards are a sharing of God's character and all that this involves. The question of course, is what does sharing God's character entail, that is, what does it mean to participate in God as the final purpose of a holy life? Over the course of this book, I have tried to offer some answers to this question. I believe that holiness is about our flourishing as human beings. Flourishing is nothing less than achieving our complete potential as human beings. We cannot achieve this potential on our own, nor were we ever designed to do so. God created us in his image, which suggests that God made us to achieve our potential as we participate in his life. With this in mind, let's consider some of the blessings that come as we share God's own life.

The first blessing of participation is stability. While it may seem like stability is not a blessing, we need to think otherwise. At this point, our lives are characterized by instability. We are buffeted by the winds of change constantly. Events and circumstances remain outside of our control. We experience sickness and death. We spend a lifetime getting to know people, developing friends, loving our spouse, pouring our lives into our children, all to have the people we love slowly ripped away from us. We crave stability even while we experience nothing but instability.

I remember when I spoke at my uncle's funeral in Florida. As I was preparing for my ten-minute eulogy, it suddenly dawned on me that the people in my life who I had come to count on were beginning to slip away. As a child, I viewed my uncle and others as stable forces in my life. They were people I could look to and count on. With my uncle's death, I realized that these people were leaving me. In one moment, I caught a glimpse of my future. One day, everything I held dear in this world would be gone. All my friends, my family would finally be taken and I would be left with nothing. As if that were not enough to endure, one day I will breathe my last breath and say goodbye to this world. No matter how much I scratch and claw at life, I cannot even hang on to my own existence. Like everything else, it too will leave me. There is instability all around. When I think in this way, I glimpse what Ecclesiastes means by vanity, vanity, all is vanity. Everything we do seems to be in vain in light of the constant instability we face.

I truly believe that we cannot begin to understand what God is giving us unless we look death square in the face and see it for what it is: the final enemy. Death is the ultimate end of instability. It is the loss of all things. There is a kind of terror associated with death because we know deep down what it means. Although we spend a lifetime building a home and making our way in the world, it will all be stripped away. This is true for the rich and the poor, the president and the panhandler. All the instability death brings can create intense fear leading to paranoia. We try desperately to hang on to what we've got. All of our cautious behavior, watching the kids closely, being careful when we drive, will be in vain. Death is the final enemy that strips humans of their very dignity by ripping life out from under them.

There is another dimension to our instability and that is the unstable nature of our character. We wish that we could be stable in all that we do. We always want to make the right choices and to be dependable. However, we realize how inconsistent we are in our behavior. We fail others all the time. In addition, we fail ourselves when we make self-destructive choices. Whenever we say to ourselves, "why did I do that!?!," we are recognizing how unstable our character is. Of course, some are more consistent than others. In the end, though, we all experience the instability of our character because no one makes the right choices all the time.

In the face of our final enemy, we must remember that the life of God is slowly renewing us day by day. As Paul declares, "even though our outer nature is wasting away, our inner nature is being renewed day by day" (2 Cor. 4:16). One day we will be clothed with God's own instability. The immortality and incorruption of God's own life will be given to us. How do we know this? The same Spirit of life who raised Jesus from the dead is our guarantee that the life of God is pouring forth into our lives. Christians need not fear the instability of life because we know that this mortality will put on immortality. This does not mean that death, pain and dying are unreal, but it does mean that they are defeated. In addition, Christians should recognize that God is slowly giving us the stability of an incorruptible life. One day we will no longer sin; we will no longer make self-destructive choices; we will be like God who always does the right thing.

The second blessing of participation is beauty. Complete perfection entails perfect beauty. The beauty of perfection is absolute poetry in motion where everything is in harmony, order and at rest. Some persons may think that at the end of all things, believers will simply cease from activity as though the beauty of perfection will end in the heavenly equivalent of a day at the beach where the believer is simply sitting and soaking up the divine rays of love. This is how they interpret the teaching of Hebrews that a final rest awaits the people of God (Heb. 4:1-11). Such a view could not be further from the truth. As Harold Attridge suggests, the teaching of Hebrews remains contingent upon the idea of Sabbath rest.[8] Sabbath is

---

8. See Attridge, *Hebrews*, 130-31.

not a time of inactivity but involves celebration and praise. At the very least, this tells us that entering into God's rest will mean a continuous state of activity. The beauty of perfection is activity and rest at the same time.

To explain what I mean, let me return to Hebrews for a moment. In Hebrews 4:3, the writer declares that "we who have believed *are entering* that rest... " (my emphasis). The verb "entering" is in the present tense suggesting that there is some sense in which believers are now participating in the rest of God. God's divine rest is not merely a future reality but must be experienced in some way now.[9] To make certain that his readers don't misunderstand him, the writer of Hebrews almost immediately says, "let us make every effort to enter that rest... " (4:11). Consequently, Hebrews tells its readers that they are entering their future rest now, but the full entrance into that rest will occur at some point in the future. This ought to tell us that Hebrews is not describing a place like the promised land was a place of rest for the Israelites. Instead, the idea of rest is bound up with the picture of salvation that Hebrews is trying to paint for us. Believers have entered salvation but have not completed it yet.

A complete understanding of rest depends upon the way Hebrews understands salvation. Believers enter their rest fully when they are fully saved. For Hebrews, this means

9. Ibid., 126; see also David A. DeSilva, *Perseverance in Gratitude: A Socio-Rhetorical Commentary on the Epistle "to the Hebrews"* (Grand Rapids, MI: Eerdmans, 2000), 155-56.

entering fully into God's presence. As we saw earlier, Jesus opens the way into God's presence through his own death on the cross. In fact, Hebrews calls Christ the "pioneer" or "captain" of our salvation (2:10; 6:20; 12:2), which suggests that Jesus is the model who both opens the way to God's presence and shows us how to enter that presence. The writer leaves little doubt as to how Jesus enters the presence of God. He is perfected by suffering (2:10) or learns obedience through suffering such that he is brought to perfection (5:7-10). As a result, the writer declares that God has a Son "who has been made perfect forever" (7:28).[10] During his earthly ministry, Jesus labored at doing the will of God and experienced the sufferings and toils of this labor. It was this process that brought Jesus to completion or perfection. As the model for believers, Jesus shows us that our laboring *now* involves a process of transformation that will lead to our perfection *then* as we enter fully into God's presence and experience God's own life. The fact that our consciences have been cleansed tells us that we have already entered God's presence even if we must labor to enter completely.

Entering the presence of God is a process of transformation that requires growth in holiness. Believers must work and labor in the same way that Jesus worked and labored. Our present work and labor involves toil and sweat.

---

10. Ibid., 197-99; D. Peterson, *Hebrews and Perfection*, 74-103; *and the People of God: Essays in Honor of Gordon D. Fee on the Occasion of His 65th Birthday*, ed. Sven K. Soderlund S. K. Soderlund and N. T. Wright (Grand Rapids, MI: Eerdmans, 1999).

That is, it's not always very fun. Earthly labor is a tiring and taxing activity that takes it out of a person even if the activity itself is ultimately beneficial. Any person who has endured the long, hard hours of learning to play an instrument or a sport knows that these labor intensive times are difficult. Yet, the long hours of practice transform the person from someone who cannot play to someone who can. When the person finally develops all the skill necessary to play well, that person can be said to have completed the learning process. In a sense, she has "finished the course" because she has moved beyond a learner and become a master of her craft.

Once the learning process is complete, the person does not cease from activity, but she does enter a new phase of activity. When Jesus enters into the presence of God, the writer of Hebrews does not have him cease from all activity. He stands at the right hand of the Father as a faithful high priest who ever lives to make intercession for the saints (Heb. 7:24-25; 12:2). How then is this activity restful? It is restful because it no longer involves the labor and toil of arriving at perfection. Instead, this activity is the fruit of a perfected life. The beauty of perfection is complete motion and stillness, activity and rest. Consider for a moment the musician who is at the peak of her craft. When she is on stage and playing, she is engaged in activity and yet her activity seems effortless. There is no toil or labor at what she does, but she is now experiencing the benefit of all her prior work. Likewise, when Sandy Koufax was pitching the perfect game, he was engaged in constant activity but it was not tiresome. After the game, Koufax said that his arm actually got stronger as he pitched. Even with these earthly activities, we can see that there comes a point where we move beyond labor and toil to the experience of rest right in the midst of what we're doing. Like the humming bird beats its wings in a rapid motion and yet remains still, so we enter a new phase where we remain active and yet experience rest.

When we fully participate in the beauty of God's perfection, we will experience what it means to work without labor, to be active and rested at the same time. The beauty of perfection is when we reflect divine poetry in motion where everything is working so harmoniously that we simply relax and enjoy. If you have ever been engaged in an activity where all of a sudden you stopped thinking about what you were doing and simply enjoyed the activity itself, then you have an idea of what life will be like when we enter God's presence. There are no worries about making mistakes, no effort at sustaining concentration. Instead, what we do will be so natural to us that it will seem like we're not doing anything at all. This is the blessing of participating in beauty of God's perfection.

The third blessing of participation is love. This is the happy ending to the story. The beloved gets her lover, the bride finally possesses her bridegroom and in so doing gains all she could ever desire. The consummation of holiness finds its ultimate expression in the embrace of two lovers who have been separated for far too long. As Christians in the Middle Ages knew all too well the Song of Songs adequately sums up the Christian life: a full embrace of her lover by the beloved. We must be careful here not to allow ourselves to become sidetracked by too literal a perception of what this means. Modern society has so shaped our understanding of sexual relations that we fail to understand what is involved in such an encounter. Human beings are sexual not simply to engage in a physical exchange but to enter into fully an intimate activity of giving and receiving, which itself is reflective of the inner life of God as a communion of love.

God exists as a communion of love. The Father, the Son and the Holy Spirit all give and receive love from one another. Theologians have described this give and take of love as the divine dance. When God invites us to share his life, he is inviting us to enter the dance of love between Father, Son and Holy Spirit. This is ultimately what it means to be the bride of Christ. Remember the bride is not one believer, but the host of the redeemed who are joined in union with Father, Son and Holy Spirit. Consequently, the dance I am describing is not a dance between each believer and God, but between all believers and God. All believers are caught up in that divine embrace where the Father, the Son and the Holy Spirit take their hands and ushering them into the joy of God's own life. To dance is to be taken up, raptured if you will, in the all-encompassing, over-whelming, indescribable joy of the presence of the triune Godhead, who unifies all things in Christ Jesus! As C. S. Lewis states,

> It is only in our 'hours off,' only in our moments of permitted festivity, that we find an analogy [for the end]. Dance and game *are* frivolous, unimportant down here; for 'down here' is not their natural place. Here, they are a moment's rest from the life we were placed here to live. But in this world everything is upside down. That which, if it could be prolonged here, would be a truancy, is like that which in a better country is the End of Ends. Joy is the serious business of Heaven.[11]

The final blessing of participation is happiness. I hope by now that you can see how our happiness and joy will arise naturally from the beauty of perfection and our participation in the divine dance. Indeed, I would suggest that we experience the beauty of poetry in motion precisely as we take our place in the divine dance. Augustine says that only God is to be enjoyed properly speaking. To draw nearer to God is to enjoy divine bliss in ever increasing measure. This bliss is described variously in scripture but most aptly put as "joy unspeakable and full of glory." Paul exhausts his supply of superlatives to express the inexpressible. By focusing upon

---

[11] C. S. Lewis, *Letters to Malcolm: Chiefly on Prayer*, (San Diego: Harvest, 1964), 93.

the rules of a holy life, we can forget its true purpose. God does not provides rules for the sake of rules. How morbid! Holiness is not about how well one performs but moving onward and upward toward perfect happiness. Our goal is the complete and utter joy that comes from experiencing the divine dance of Father, Son and Holy Spirit. It is a joy that arises naturally from our own activity, when we enter into a place of rest from the weariness of our labors and simply experience the joy of doing something. If the goal is the complete joy that comes from God himself, one can understand why Paul would declare that he presses on toward the mark of the high calling in Christ Jesus.

For Our Sakes He Became Poor

In drawing our discussion to a close, we need to listen once again to the angels' song of the sweet silent night, the holy night into which the eternal Word of God first entered our life that he might invite us to enter his. The song that the angels sing is a new song. It is God's concerto where the first verse begins "Glory to God in the highest and on earth, peace and good will toward men" and the last verse concludes "To him who sits on the throne and unto the Lamb be blessing and glory and honor forever and ever." In the first verse, we see the announcement of God's taking upon himself our poverty. Our poverty becomes his poverty. As Paul declares, "for your sakes he became poor" (2 Cor. 8:9). This is the movement of divinity toward humanity. When God became a human being, he willingly bankrupted himself not only entering into the fragility of human existence but going to the margins of that existence, the forgotten and forsaken side of life. For the God of life intends to bring life to the deepest darkest places of the world. In the final verse of the song, we see all of creation joining to bless the God who has blessed them and made them partakers of his life. This is the movement of humanity toward divinity. When God became a man, he led humanity on a new exodus out of sin, death and judgment not simply to a new life but to his life--a life of holiness and happiness.

Imagine arriving at a place where we no longer sabotage ourselves by our words and deeds. Those personality traits that work against us are gone. It's one person's tendency to get angry over little things that then causes him to do or say something he regrets. Or, it's another person's insecurities about herself, which cause her not to risk and say something or do something she knows she should. It's the guilt one person wrongly feels for doing something he knows is the right thing to do. It's the perfectionism that prompts another to question everything she does as never being good enough. We never can seem to get over these traits; they dog us like a ball and chain wrapped around our necks from which we cannot seem to break free. And yet, God invites us to begin a journey that will culminate in our complete liberation from these self-destructive tendencies. He beckons us to come with him and enter the path of holiness.

For our sakes the eternal Son became poor that we might become rich. The incarnate God experienced his first human breath that we might breathe the air of heaven; he covered himself in the impoverished and abandoned scent of an unclean stable that we might be bathed in the aroma of his majesty and glory; he clothed himself in the frailty of human flesh that we might put on the garment of his power and might. He has taken human flesh to lead humanity to its true home. This home is not simply a place. We would miss the true significance of salvation if we were to see it simply as acquiring a mansion on some hillside. Heaven is heaven because of God. It is the reflection of God's own beauty. We too will reflect that beauty as we join the dance around the throne.

> *Beulah land, I'm longing for you,*
> *And some day on thee I'll stand,*
> *There my home shall be eternal*
> *Beulah land, sweet Beulah land*

Bibliography

Adler, Mortimer J. *Aristotle for Everybody: Difficult Thought Made Easy.* New York, NY: Macmillan, 1978.

Anselm, Saint, *Archbishop of Canterbury, 1033-1109. St. Anselm's Proslogion.* Oxford: Clarendon Press, 1965.

Aquinas, Thomas. *Summa Theologiae.* trans. Fathers of the Dominican Allen, TX: Christian Classics, 1948.

Attridge, Harold W. *Hebrews.* (Hermeneia: A Critical and Historical Commentary on the Bible) Philadelphia, PA: Fortress Press, 1989.

Augustine, *The Confessions of St. Augustine: Books I-X,* Kansas City: Sheed Andrews and McMeel, 1970.

Barth, Karl, Geoffrey W. Bromiley, and Thomas F. Torrance. *Church Dogmatics,* Vol. 2, Part 1-2. Edinburgh: T & T Clark, 1957.

_____. *Evangelical Theology: An Introduction.* trans. Grand Rapids, MI: Eerdmans, 1979.

Bauckham, R. *The Climax of Prophecy: Studies on the Book of Revelation.* Edinburgh: T & T Clark, 1993.

_____. *The Theology of the Book of Revelation.* Cambridge: Cambridge University Press, 1993.

Bauckham, Richard. *The Climax of Prophecy: Studies on the Book of Revelation.* Edinburgh: T & T Clark, 1993.

Berquist, Jon L. *Judaism in Persia's Shadow: A Social and Historical Approach.* Minneapolis, MN: Fortress Press, 1995.

Blenkinsopp, J. *Isaiah 40-55.* The Anchor Bible New York, NY: Doubleday, 2000.

_____. *Isaiah 1-39.* The Anchor Bible, vol. 19 New York, NY: Doubleday, 2000.

Bonhoeffer, Dietrich. *The Cost of Discipleship,* second edition, trans. R. H. Fuller New York, NY: Macmillan Publishing, 1959.

231

Brown, William P. *Character in Crisis: A Fresh Approach to the Wisdom Literature of the Old Testament*. Grand Rapids, MI: Eerdmans, 1996.

Brueggemann, Walter. *Theology of the Old Testament: Testimony, Dispute, Advocacy*. Minneapolis, MN: Fortress Press, 1997.

Bunyan, John. *Grace Abounding to the Chief of Sinners*. Menston: Scolar P, 1970.

Charry, Ellen T. *By the Renewing of Your Minds: The Pastoral Function of Christian Doctrine*. New York, NY: Oxford University Press, 1997.

Chester, Andrew and Ralph P. Martin, *The Theology of the Letters of James, Peter, and Jude*. Cambridge: Cambridge University Press, 1994.

Clements, R. E. *Wisdom in Theology*. The Didsbury Lectures, 1989, Grand Rapids, MI: Eerdmans, 1992.

Collins, Kenneth J. *The Scripture Way of Salvation: The Heart of John Wesley's Theology*. Nashville, TN: Abingdon Press, 1997.

Delaney, J. J. *The Practice of the Presence of God*. trans. New York, NY: Doubleday, 1996.

DeSilva, David A. *Perseverance in Gratitude: A Socio-Rhetorical Commentary on the Epistle "to the Hebrews."* Grand Rapids, MI: Eerdmans, 2000.

DiFalco, Teresa. *Review of Sandy Koufax: A Lefty's Legacy*, by Jane Leavy, PopMatters Online. <http://www.popmatters.com/books/reviews/s/sandy-koufax.shtml> Retrieved 16 February 2004.

Dunn, James D. G. "Spirit Speech: Reflections on Romans 8:12-27" in *Romans and the People of God: Essays in Honor of Gordon D. Fee on the Occasion of His 65th Birthday*, Sven K. Soderlund and N. T. Wright eds., Grand Rapids, MI: Eerdmans, 1999.

_____. *The Theology of Paul the Apostle*. Grand Rapids, MI: Eerdmans, 1998.

Fee, Gordon. *God's Empowering Presence: The Holy Spirit in the Letters of Paul*. Peabody, MA: Hendrickson Publishers, 1994.

_____. *The First Epistle to the Corinthians*. New International Commentary on the New Testament, Grand Rapids, MI: Eerdmans, 1987.

_____. *Paul, the Spirit and the People of God*. Peabody, MA: Hendrickson, 1996.

Ferguson, Sinclair. *John Owen on the Christian Life*. Edinburgh: The Banner of Truth Trust, 1987.

Foster, Richard. *Prayer: Finding the Heart's True Home* ((New York, NY: HarperOne, 2003).

Hauerwas, Stanley. *A Community of Character: Toward a Constructive Christian Social Ethic* Notre Dame: University of Notre Dame Press, 1981.

_____. *The Peaceable Kingdom: A Primer in Christian Ethics*. Notre Dame: University of Notre Dame Press, 1983.

Hollis, Gause, R. *Revelation: God's Stamp of Sovereignty on History*. Cleveland, TN: Pathway Press, 1983.

Hunsinger, George. *How to Read Karl Barth: The Shape of His Theology*. New York, NY: Oxford University Press, 1991.

Hurtado, Larry W. *Lord Jesus Christ: Devotion to Jesus in Earliest Christianity*. Grand Rapids, MI: Eerdmans, 2003.

Johnson, Luke Timothy. *Reading Romans: A Literary and Theological Commentary*. New York, NY: Crossroad Publishing Co., 1997.

Leavy, Jane. "Conversation: Lefty's Legacy," interview by Terence Smith, *The NewsHour* October 21, 2002. <http://www.pbs.org/newshour/conversation/July-dec02/leavy_10-21.html> Retrieved 17 February 2004.

Marshall, Ian Howard. *1 Peter*. Downers Grove, IL: InterVarsity Press, 1991.

McGrath, Alister E. *Reformation Thought: An Introduction*. Oxford: Blackwell Publishers, 1999.

Murphy-O'Connor, J. *The Theology of the Second Letter to the Corinthians*. Cambridge: Cambridge University Press, 1991.

Owen, J. *Sin and Temptation: The Challenge to Personal Godliness*. Portland, OR: Multnomah Press, 1983.

Peterson, David A. *Hebrews and Perfection: An Examination of the Concept of Perfection in the Epistle to the Hebrews*. Cambridge: Cambridge University Press, 1982.

Philips, J. B. *Your God is Too Small*. New York: The Macmillan Company, 1965.

Plantinga, Cornelius J. *Not the Way It's Supposed to Be*: A Breviary of Sin. Grand Rapids, MI: Eerdmans, 1995.

Rowley, H. H. *The Biblical Doctrine of Election*. London: Lutterworth Press, 1950.

Sproul, R. C. *Chosen By God*. Wheaton, IL: Tyndale House Publishers, 1986.

Staupitz, Johann. "Eternal Predestination and its Execution in Time" in *Forerunners of the Reformation: The Shape of Late Medieval Thought*. Heiko Oberman, ed., Philadelphia, PA: Fortress Press, 1981.

Stedman, Ray C. *Body Life*. Glendale, CA: Regal Books, 1972.

Stuart, Douglas. *Hosea – Jonah*. Word Biblical Commentary 31, Waco, TX: Word Books, 1987.

Wesley, John. *"On Working Out Your Own Salvation" in John Wesley's Sermons: An Anthology*. A. C. Outler and R. P. Heitzenrater, eds., Nashville, TN: Abingdon Press, 1991.

Westermann, Claus. *Genesis 1-11: A Commentary*. trans. John J. Scullion, Minneapolis, MN: Augsburg/Fortress Press, 1984.

_____. *Roots of Wisdom: The Oldest Proverbs of Israel and Other Peoples*. trans. J. Daryl Charles, Louisville, KY: John Knox Press, 1995.

Wolff, H. W. *Anthropology of the Old Testament*. trans. Margaret Kohl, Philadelphia, PA: Fortress Press, 1974.

WOW Worship Songbook: Today's 30 Most Powerful Worship Songs. Mobile, AL: Integrity Incorporated, 2000.

Wright, N. T. *"New Exodus, New Inheritance: The Narrative Substructure of Romans 3-8"* in *Romans and the People of God: Essays in Honor of Gordon D. Fee.* Grand Rapids, MI: Eerdmans, 1999.

Ziesler, J. A. *Pauline Christianity.* Oxford: Oxford University Press, 1990.

_____. *Paul's Letter to the Romans,* TPI New Testament Commentaries, Philadelphia, PA: Trinity Press International, 1989.

Index

236

CPSIA information can be obtained
at www.ICGtesting.com
Printed in the USA
BVHW041638040621
608825BV00004B/1242

9 781938 373565